3 95

P9-DMH-268

Clarifying Values
Through Subject Matter

Applications for the Classroom

Clarifying Values Through Subject Matter

Applications for the Classroom

Merrill Harmin
Howard Kirschenbaum
Sidney B. Simon

Copyright © 1973 by Winston Press, Inc.
Library of Congress Catalog Card Number: 73-75299
ISBN: 0-03-008241-2
Printed in the United States of America

9 8 7 6 5

Winston Press
430 Oak Grove
Minneapolis, Minnesota 55403

Acknowledgments

Grateful acknowledgment is given for permission to reprint the following excerpts from copyrighted materials:

From *The Process of Education* by Jerome S. Bruner. Reprinted by permission of Harvard University Press. © 1960.

From *Summerhill: A Radical Approach to Child Rearing* by A. S. Neill. Copyright 1960 Hart Publishing Company, New York. Used by permission.

From *Teaching as a Subversive Activity* by Neil Postman and Charles Weingartner. Used with permission of Delacorte Press. © 1969.

From *Experience and Education* by John Dewey, The Kappa Delta Pi Lecture Series. Copyright 1938, by Kappa Delta Pi. Used by permission of Kappa Delta Pi, An Honor Society in Education, owners of the copyright.

"The Road Not Taken" by Robert Frost. From THE POETRY OF ROBERT FROST edited by Edward Connery Lathem. Copyright 1916, © 1969 by Holt, Rinehart and Winston, Inc. Copyright 1944 by Robert Frost. Reprinted by permission of Holt, Rinehart and Winston, Inc.

Table of Contents

THE FUNCTION OF INFORMATION IS TO INFORM.

TO INFORM WHAT?

TO INFORM YOUR VALUES.

—Louis E. Raths

1

A Call
For Change

...What avail is it to win prescribed amounts of information about geography and history, to win ability to read and write, if in the process the individual loses his own soul: loses his appreciation of things worth while, of the values to which these are relative; if he loses desire to apply what he has learned and, above all, loses the ability to extract meaning from his future experiences as they occur?

Experience and Education
by John Dewey (8)*

*Numbers in parentheses refer to publications listed in the Bibliography at the end of the book.

...Education should be a preparation for life. Our culture has not been very successful. Our education, politics, and economics lead to war....Our religion has not abolished usury and robbery....The advances of the age are advances in mechanism—in radio and television, in electronics, in jet planes. New world wars threaten, for the world's social conscience is still primitive....Why does man hate and kill in war when animals do not?...Why are there so many suicides?... Why the hate that is anti-Semitism? Why Negro hating and lynching?...Why, a thousand whys about our vaunted state of civilized eminence!

I ask these questions because I am by profession a teacher, one who deals with the young. I ask these questions because those so often asked by teachers are the unimportant ones, the ones about school subjects. I ask what earthly good can come out of discussions about French or ancient history or what not when these subjects don't matter a jot compared to the larger question of life's natural fulfillment—of man's inner happiness.

Summerhill: A Radical Approach to Child Rearing
by A. S. Neill (28)

At a time when our students need desperately a bitter dose of reality, the curriculum makers turn out a homogenized pap—bland, insipid, innocuous, and deadly dull....One could search all the curriculum projects in vain for evidence that they were written... at a time when our cities are suffocating in their own effluvia and when our towns are being torn by riots.

Allan A. Glatthorn
from a speech to the National Association
of Secondary School Principals, 1968

...it is not beyond our ingenuity to design school environments which can help young people to master concepts necessary to survival in a rapidly changing world. The institution we call "school" is what it is because we made it that way. If it is irrelevant, as Marshall McLuhan says; if it shields children from reality, as Norbert Wiener says; if it educates for obsolescence, as John Gardner says;...if it is based on fear, as John Holt says; if it avoids the promotion of significant learnings, as Carl Rogers says; if it induces alienation, as Paul Goodman says; if it punishes creativity and independence, as Edgar Friedenberg says; if, in short, it is not doing what needs to be done, it can be changed; it *must* be changed.

Teaching as a Subversive Activity
by Neil Postman and Charles Weingartner (29)

Much has been written about the need for change in the educational system. Yet systems are hard to change.

Clarifying Values through Subject Matter offers one approach for making classrooms more relevant to a world of change, confusion, and conflict. It is not the only approach needed, but it is a practical one—something the teacher can use on Monday.

Clarifying values through subject matter is a relatively simple method for the teacher to implement in his or her classroom; yet its implications are, we think, revolutionary.

The Authors

Three Levels
Of Teaching

Almost every subject in our schools can be taught on any or all of three levels: 1) the facts level, 2) the concepts level, and 3) the values level.*

Education at the facts level includes the teaching and learning of specific information, facts, details, occurrences, events, and actualities. It also includes the basic rudiments in learning a skill: for example, the meanings of words, the fingering of a musical instrument, or the fundamentals of penmanship.

At the concepts level, teachers and students explore the principles behind the facts. The learner groups isolated facts together in order to make generalizations from the data he has gathered. Abstractions and ideas are entertained. Where skills are involved, the more complicated processes of the skill are learned and practiced. For example, the student who has learned the rudiments of a musical instrument will now learn to perform whole pieces with appropriate dynamics, tempo, and intonation.

On the values level, students relate the facts and concepts of a subject area to their own lives. The values

*Although there are many other ways of conceptualizing subject matter (3, 7, 26), those systems will not be discussed.

level raises that scary question "What does this have to do with me?" a necessary question for students to ask if they are to derive personal meaning from subject matter. At this level, students explore the connection between the subject matter and their own feelings, opinions, and behavior.

To distinguish between the three levels of teaching, the Pilgrim story will be used, since it is familiar to all of us.

PILGRIM STORY—FACTS

To review briefly, the Pilgrims fled England to escape religious intolerance and persecution and settled in Holland where they were free to worship as they chose. In Holland, learning a new language and adapting to a new culture was difficult for them. Some of the Pilgrims feared the loss of their ethnic identity. Therefore, they decided to establish their own community in the New World. Embarking on the ship Mayflower, about one hundred men, women, and children departed from Southampton for unknown shores. In 1620, they landed at Plymouth Harbor. There the winter was harsh, and half of the immigrants perished. In the spring, with the help of neighboring Indians, the Pilgrims planted their first crop. By fall the harvest was rich and abundant. To celebrate their survival and the harvest, the Pilgrims invited the Indians to a feast—the first Thanksgiving. (And to include a part of the story often omitted—although the Pilgrims fled to a new land in search of freedom to worship God in their own way, their descendants did not extend religious freedom to others. Several years later the clergyman Roger Williams was banished because his religious beliefs differed from theirs.)

To discover what facts the children have learned about the Pilgrim story, the teacher asks these kinds of questions:

- Why did the Pilgrims leave England?

- What problems did they encounter in Holland? What problems did they encounter on the Mayflower?

- How did they learn to survive in the wilderness? How did the Indians help them?

- Name four of the important Pilgrim leaders and describe their contribution to American history.

- The Pilgrims signed an agreement with each other called the Mayflower Compact. True or false.

- Circle the date when the Pilgrims landed in America: 1492, 1609, 1620, 1654.

- Why did the Pilgrims celebrate the first Thanksgiving? Whom did they invite as guests?

- The descendants of the Pilgrims did not extend religious freedom to others. True or false.

- What eventually happened to Roger Williams?

The chart below highlights the facts level of the Pilgrim story.

THE PILGRIM STORY

Facts Level

England/Roger Williams
Holland
Mayflower
Plymouth Rock
Friendly Indians
First Thanksgiving

Concepts Level

Values Level

PILGRIM STORY — CONCEPTS

Moving from the facts to the concepts level in the Pilgrim story, a class examines significant historical themes such as "prejudice" and "emigration" and relates these themes to past and current history. Students analyze and interpret the facts of the Pilgrim story. They engage in activities such as role playing to help them experience what the Pilgrims faced. Upon the historical facts of the Pilgrim story, they build generalizations, abstractions, and, finally, concepts which are common to the history of man.

Here are some typical concept questions that teachers or students might ask:

Prejudice: What is prejudice? What are some examples of prejudice today? What does it do to people? Why does prejudice exist? How is it that people who have experienced prejudice against themselves can still be prejudiced against others? How can prejudice be fought? (The students might role-play a scene in England in which the Pilgrims are the targets of intolerance.)

Cultural Assimilation: What is cultural assimilation? Can you think of other examples of cultural assimilation in world history? What different ethnic groups live in your community? Is America really a "melting pot"? What are the advantages and disadvantages of cultural assimilation?

12

Emigration: What are the different reasons people might move from one place to another? Can you think of other examples in world history when entire peoples or large groups emigrated? Is there any difference between Pilgrims and refugees? (Note: When answers to questions like these are given by the teacher and memorized by the students, the class is still working on the facts level.)

Wilderness/Civilization: How do we decide which of these terms to apply to a society? What advantages does civilization have over wilderness? Wilderness over civilization? What is necessary for survival? (The class might go on a weekend camping trip, planning the activities and arranging for the supplies they would need to survive.)

Helping: What qualities are found in a good, helping relationship? Why do some people find it hard to ask for help? What can a helper do to make it easier for the other person to accept his help? Are there times when it is best not to help? When? What organizations in our community are devoted to "helping"?

Ritual/Ceremony: Why do we continue to celebrate Thanksgiving? What does man gain from ceremonies and rituals? How do they become outdated? Can you list twenty other rituals performed in our society?

Now the chart includes some of the major concepts implicit in the Pilgrim story.

THE PILGRIM STORY

Facts Level

    England/Roger Williams
    Holland
    Mayflower
    Plymouth Rock
    Friendly Indians
    First Thanksgiving

Concepts Level

    Prejudice
    Cultural Assimilation
    Emigration
    Wilderness/Civilization
    Helping
    Ritual/Ceremony

Values Level

PILGRIM STORY—VALUES

A teacher working with values questions uses the pronoun "you" to directly involve students, urging them to relate the subject matter to their own lives. The teacher will employ this form of questioning repeatedly, encouraging students to think, to clarify, to affirm.

Here are some typical questions a teacher asks to extend the study of the Pilgrims to the values level:

Prejudice: Have *you* ever experienced prejudice? What was the situation? Would you react any differently today? Do *you* have a prejudice for or against something or someone? How do you think these prejudices originated? Are you glad you have any of these prejudices? If you changed one of your prejudices, what other beliefs might change with it? Have *you* ever tried to combat prejudice? What were the results?

Cultural Assimilation: What is *your* ethnic background? Are you proud of it? What is one thing you are proud of about the ethnic group you were born into? What is one thing you are not proud of? Have you ever visited a foreign country or been in a group which didn't speak your language? How did you feel? Who are the strangers in your community or country today? Can you think of anything *you* could do to help them feel more at home?

Emigration: Is there anything *you* feel so strongly about that, if it were taken from you, you would want to leave this country? Think of the people you would really want to say goodbye to if you were to leave this country forever. How many people did you think of? How would you say goodbye to them? The Pilgrims couldn't take their belongings with them. If you could take only one suitcase with you, what do you prize so much that you would put it in the suitcase?

Wilderness/Civilization: Do *you* ever want to get away from all civilization? How much time would you like to spend in the wilderness? How self-sufficient are you? Make a list of electrical appliances you could do without for a month. Six months. What in *you* is still savage and untamed like the wilderness? Do you like it? What is civilized in you that you like or don't like?

Helping: Can you think of a recent time *you* tried to help someone? How was the help received? Would you offer it any differently today? Rank these four items in order of difficulty for *you:* offering help, helping, asking for help, receiving help. What feelings do you have when you ask for help?

Ritual/Ceremony: What do *you* give deep thanks for? To whom do you give the thanks? What are some of the rituals we practice in school? Which rituals have meaning for you? Which don't? What is a ceremony or ritual in your life that you'd like to see eliminated? Is there something in life you'd like to see celebrated or remembered? Can you create a new ritual or ceremony that would celebrate it? Would you consider practicing this new ritual?

Now the chart is complete at all three levels.

THE PILGRIM STORY

Facts Level

England/Roger Williams
Holland
Mayflower
Plymouth Rock
Friendly Indians
First Thanksgiving

Concepts Level

Prejudice
Cultural Assimilation
Emigration
Wilderness/Civilization
Helping
Ritual/Ceremony

Values Level

YOU
YOU
YOU
YOU
YOU
YOU

Teaching on All Three Levels

Human beings enter learning at the facts level. From birth, we are continuously bombarded with stimuli from the world outside our bodies and with feelings and sensations from within. We sense, we observe, we perceive—we absorb an enormous amount of information. To survive, we attempt to make sense out of all these stimuli, all these facts.

As we do this, we move to the next level of learning, the concepts level. We generalize about our observations. We begin to form and use abstractions and ideas which help us to think and to communicate. We find meaning in the myriad perceptions and observations we have made.

Our search for cognitive meaning, however, remains primarily an intellectual exercise, unless, somehow, it is lived out in life. Thus, we enter the third level of learning, the values level, where the meanings we have made are profound enough to change our attitudes, our behaviors, and our lives.

In our schools, students are usually taught at the facts or concepts level. Sometimes at both. Rarely are students taught at the facts, concepts, *and* values level, although the most successful education includes all three. The following pages attempt to explain why.

18

THE FACTS LEVEL

Facts and basic skills are among the building blocks of the educational enterprise. We need to know the meaning of words and symbols—how to read, write, add, and subtract. A knowledge of "the facts" is the first step in making sense of our world. History cannot be charted without facts. Mathematical and scientific concepts are based on facts. Without facts, we cannot generalize, conceptualize, or make abstractions. Facts are necessary if we are to build a viable set of values, unbiased by group opinion or unprejudiced by personal attitudes.

Teaching on the facts level alone may have certain advantages over teaching on the other levels. For example, a test based on facts or basic skills can be more objective than a test based on concepts and values. Structuring learning programs is less complicated on the facts level. Teaching on the facts level provides a way of setting standards and norms and assures a common language and background for all who attend school.

However, teaching on the facts level alone has serious drawbacks. Primarily, the facts level involves memory work; it requires few of the higher levels of thinking and includes little relation to the life experience of students. Teachers who employ only facts seldom integrate them with other aspects of the subject matter. Facts remain isolated—bits of knowledge to be memorized for an exam and then discarded. Although occasionally interesting, facts by themselves rarely touch the individual or his life in any significant way.

Rote memorization of concepts or generalizations is simply more facts-level learning. It is possible for students to memorize any concept without really understanding it—for example, Thoreau's concept of a philosopher:

> To be a philosopher is not merely to have subtle thoughts, nor even to found a school, but so to love wisdom as to live according to its dictates, a life of simplicity, independence, magnanimity and trust.

Students could memorize Thoreau's concept without the slightest notion of what he meant. Similarly, teachers often convey mathematical concepts—multiplication, division, fractions—in rote fashion. When teachers introduce concepts in this manner, they are still teaching at the facts level.

Teaching facts alone does not allow a student to develop thinking ability or creativity. Nor do facts alone enrich the affective (emotional) and valuing areas of his life.

Historical Changes

Yet, for years many educators have demanded more than memorization from their students. As far back as the 1930s, some educators broke from the fact- and memorization-centered approach to teaching and moved to a problem-centered approach. They hoped to make learning more relevant to the lives of their students by encouraging them to solve problems

20

of concern to them. In this way, students would learn not only facts, but hopefully such skills as the techniques of research, self-discipline, and cooperative problem solving. Under John Dewey, for instance, students began with an interest in flax and ended up investigating the history of civilization.

Followers of Dewey furthered the problem-centered approach by focusing on social issues—juvenile delinquency, race relations, urban planning, war, and peace. However, this approach, while popular for a brief period, never achieved mass support and gradually diminished in use. (It is interesting to note that it seems to be gaining renewed interest in recent years.)

Then, in the late fifties and early sixties, many educators again tried to encourage a structured teaching approach that extended beyond the level of facts. Within this movement, students approached a discipline just as a scholar in the same field might approach his tasks. Scholars and technical experts assisted in creating curricula which emphasized the *structure* of the subject—the skills, methods, and processes needed to inquire into the fundamental concepts of the subject. As Jerome Bruner explained in *The Process of Education* (7):

> ...the basic ideas that lie at the heart of
> all science and mathematics and the
> basic themes that give form to life and
> literature are as simple as they are
> powerful. To be in command of these

basic ideas, to use them effectively, requires a continual deepening of one's
understanding of them that comes from
learning to use them in progressively
more complex forms. It is only when
such basic ideas are put in formalized
terms as equations or elaborated verbal
concepts that they are out of reach of
the young child, if he has not first understood them intuitively and had a chance
to try them out on his own.

THE CONCEPTS LEVEL

Teaching on the concepts level has definite advantages over teaching on the facts level. Students who
learn the basic ideas and methods of inquiry can readily
assimilate and classify facts. They can integrate facts
into overall concepts and fundamental themes. Details
are drawn together as part of the fabric of the subject.
Students develop concepts and skills which they can
use for a lifetime, long after specific facts are forgotten.
Postman and Weingartner describe the student's role,
at this level, as being that of "meaning maker."

Lately, new teaching aids have been designed for
teaching on the concepts level. Students are encouraged to inquire independently by conducting scientific
experiments, manipulating Cuisenaire rods or balance
scales, or by building metaphors through a programmed
text. They are stimulated to be creative, to work with
basic materials, and to discover for themselves the

meaning of the concepts. In this way they test out their ideas. Mistakes are not punished or denigrated, but are thought of as part of the learning process. Students are allowed to develop at their own rate, assisting each other in their learning. In the learning process, the teacher is more a guide or facilitator than an educational dictator.

Teaching on the concepts level is widely accepted in education today. It would be difficult to question the need for "well-educated" citizens who have developed an appreciation of important concepts and who have learned the skills of inquiry.

But this is not enough.

For too long, we have allowed our educational system to rest on the questionable assumption that educated people are also happy people and moral people. We have incorrectly assumed that the ability for rational and abstract thought also enables people to make value decisions. But cognitive ability does not automatically provide people with solutions to values problems. We have seen too many people who hold college degrees, but who are unfulfilled in their own lives, their marriages, their homes, and their jobs. We have also seen brilliant scholars contribute to the destruction of human life and the physical environment because they did not consider the consequences of their work, the lives of the humans affected, or the values their work encouraged.

It is unnecessary to point to the extreme physical and moral atrocities committed by educated people and groups. To see the failure of cognitive learning, we need only observe our present social crises—in ecology, race relations, poverty, and war. Despite the voluminous reports of commissions and committees and despite our emphasis on cognitive planning, social problems have grown worse. The reports gather dust. We have not implemented the plans. We have been unable or unwilling to act quickly or broadly enough on programs that might have brought change.

Our education trains us to deal with ideas, but not with values decisions. When the concepts level places the emphasis on cognitive functions, it neglects the personal lives and feelings of students. Although teachers at this level often try to make the subject matter relevant to today's world, the issues remain at the abstract, problem-solving level. As Postman and Weingartner state, "It is almost impossible to find in Bruner's explications of inquiry learning one illustration of children's solving problems that are of deep concern to children, although most of the problems seem to interest Bruner."

It is not surprising that the critical thinking skills learned in the social studies classes or the scientific method taught and retaught in science classes or the concept of beauty taught in art, music, and literature classes so rarely carry over into students' daily lives.

THE VALUES LEVEL

If we are to make a difference in the quality of our students' lives, we cannot be content to remain on the facts and concepts levels of teaching. We must enter a third level, a values level, where subject matter is related to the lives of students—their interests, attitudes, concerns, feelings, and behaviors.

Children can learn both concepts and valuing at any age. Even a small child is capable of making concrete choices. "If you found a quarter, what would you buy?" "What games do you like to play?" As the child matures, as he acquires more knowledge, he is able to make broader choices. He can discriminate from among more complex alternatives. The complicated issues of society become more manageable for him.

When Louis E. Raths would rhetorically ask his students "What is the function of information?" the information he referred to was facts and concepts. He would continue: "The function of information is to inform. But to inform what? To inform our values." The purpose of facts and concepts, then, is to *in*form— to give form to—our values, our decisions, our daily lives.

THREE-LEVEL TEACHING

The three levels of teaching can be illustrated by the use of a pyramid.

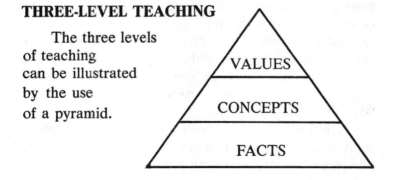

Facts serve as the foundation for the pyramid. There are billions of isolated facts. These separate facts are the building blocks from which concepts and generalizations are made. No generalization can stand unless it is supported by facts. No complicated skill can be effectively mastered unless the many separate, basic skills are mastered first.

There are many fewer concepts than there are facts. One reason why teaching on the concepts level is more useful than teaching on the facts level is because the former incorporates more information with fewer constructs. The concepts level constitutes a higher form of knowledge from which the billions of isolated facts can be viewed and organized.

There are even fewer values in our lives than concepts. They are formed from and rest upon the meanings we perceive, the concepts we have, and the generalizations we make about the world and about ourselves. Our values guide our lives. Just as teaching for concepts is richer and more useful than teaching for facts, teaching for value development is richer and more useful than teaching for concepts. Thus, the values level forms the top of the pyramid. However, without facts and concepts to support them, values are untenable. They are without meaning and are not based in reality. But based on a solid foundation of facts and concepts, values enable us to guide our lives through a complex world.

Real learning includes all three levels of development. It is, as one educator described it, "all-of-a-piece." The process of education can not be merely a cognitive exercise. To be meaningful, education must significantly touch the lives of students and integrate thinking, feeling, and acting in such a way that individuals have a sense of purpose in life. Furthermore, education should not impose meanings and values upon the individual, but rather it must help him discover cognitive and personal meanings for himself. This is the goal of teaching on all three levels of instruction: to help students discern facts, make sense of them, and finally live by the meanings they perceive.

Here is an example of three-level teaching.

A class is studying the Vietnam War on all three levels. They examine the facts: How did the war begin? What were the terms of the 1954 Geneva Agreements? Who was Ngo Dinh Diem? As the students look more closely at the facts, they inevitably make comparisons between the Vietnam War and other wars. The comparisons deepen their understanding of concepts such as aggression, liberation, revolution, oligarchy, and communism. In conducting their own research and weighing the evidence, they learn the process of historical research. On the values level, students consider the alternatives open to the United States and then weigh the consequences of each alternative. They choose personal positions on the war and publicly affirm and defend their points of view. They write letters or act on their beliefs in some appropriate way. The class has integrated the facts, concepts, and values levels.

Many teachers wonder about the ordering of the three levels. There is no simple answer. Teachers can

27

successfully begin and end on any of the levels. Yet, there is a persuasive argument for generally trying to begin and end on the values level.

If students are seeking information to solve a values problem that has importance to them, they will want to know about the facts and the concepts behind the problem. Thus by beginning on the values level, students are often more motivated to work on the other two levels. Then, once most of a unit or area of study has been completed, it seems wise to go back to the central values questions: What difference has this made in your lives? What did you learn that was important to you? What beliefs of yours have changed or become firmer? How might you live your life differently as a result of what you've learned? Starting on the values level motivates and focuses the study; ending on the values level draws together and clarifies the learnings which the students themselves find significant.

Another dilemma of three-level teaching is the amount of time to be spent on each level. Too much time on the factual level tends to dry up the mind, making study seem boring and irrelevant. Too much time on the concepts level can reduce learning to an intellectual exercise conducted in an ivory tower. On the other hand, if too much time is spent on the values level, discussion can become merely a "bull session." If it leads to any action, it is likely to lead to action that is uninformed and unconsidered.

There is no formula to tell a teacher how much time to spend on each level in a given subject area.

The teacher must himself make a value judgment about what is worth teaching. Hopefully, each teacher will decide after asking himself: How is this subject helping to inform my students' values? What difference will this really make in their lives?

Teaching on all three levels can integrate various aspects of the subject matter with the individual student's life. The student is encouraged to think, feel, and act. He builds upon his perceptions and experiences to find meaning and values. What he learns in school helps him determine the direction of his life.

The Goal of Values-Clarification

• Connie, ten years old with big brown eyes and long, dark hair, talks about herself and about her mother who is on welfare. She says, "I'd like to find out what I want to be. I'd like to find a job and earn enough money to have my own apartment and to buy a car. I don't want an expensive apartment, like for a hundred-thirty dollars a month, but one for about ten dollars. Then I could take care of my mother."

• Fourteen-year-old Tim moved from the city to a small town where he was dropped from all the school teams because he had let his hair grow long. The administration even threatens to expel him from school.

• Bill is not doing well in his inner-city school. When his mother visits the school, the teacher tells her that Bill daydreams in class. The teacher adds, "But why should you worry how he does? The boy will never get out of the ghetto anyway."

• A group of older teenagers complain about their urban neighborhood. If two or three boys congregate on the corner, the police accuse them of making trouble and threaten them. The hamburger joint on the corner kicked them out because adults complained that they made too much noise. They are welcome only in bars. There is no place else in the neighborhood where they can get together.

• Returning from a weekend at the lake, the Schmidts discover that friends of their fifteen-year-old daughter used their apartment for an unchaperoned party. Mary's friends threatened to exclude her from all their activities unless she gave them the apartment key.

These situations raise questions of values. Each situation clearly illustrates that arriving at values is a difficult, often painful, process; one that requires frequent choices between conflicting alternatives.

Too often schools supply only a knowledge of facts, concepts, or cognitive skills. Yet this knowledge is not enough to equip young people for coping with problems in today's pluralistic and complex society. Young people have become aware that their schools are failing them, and an increasing number of students are no longer willing to tolerate a curriculum that does not acknowledge their needs, interests, and concerns. Schools, as well as homes, must offer young people a way to develop a set of values upon which they can act and base their lives.

How do young people acquire a set of values? Are we to tell them what to value and how to live, over and over and over again, in the hope that they will listen? No. None of us can be certain that our values are right for other people. And even if we believed they were right, our own choices could not

31

possibly apply to all the diverse values problems and dilemmas young people will encounter. Students do not need any more values imposed upon them. They *do* need to learn the skills that will help them develop their own values. For this reason it is more effective to teach a *process of valuing* than it is to teach one set of values.

Louis E. Raths, in *Values and Teaching* (30), outlined a process of valuing composed of seven subprocesses. The subprocesses help persons of all ages to make choices which are both personally satisfying and socially responsible. As students build the total process into their lives, they need less and less to be told what is desirable or how to act.

The seven subprocesses, based on choosing, prizing, and acting, are outlined here:

CHOOSING one's beliefs and behaviors

1. *Choosing freely.*

If we are to live by our own values system, we must learn how to make independent choices. If we are able only to follow authority, we will be ineffectual when authority is silent or absent, when it gives us conflicting directions, or when our emotions impel us in contrary directions.

2. *Choosing from alternatives.*

For choice-making to have meaning, there have to be alternatives from which to choose. If there are no alternatives, there are no choices. The more alternatives available, the more likely we are to value our choices. Generating and considering alternative choices is necessary for clarifying and refining values.

3. *Choosing after thoughtful consideration of consequences.*

We need to learn to examine alternatives in terms of their expected consequences. If we don't, our choice-making is likely to be whimsical, impulsive, or conforming. By considering consequences, we lessen the chance of those consequences being unexpected or unpleasant.

PRIZING one's beliefs and behaviors

4. *Prizing and cherishing.*

Values inevitably include not only our rational choices, but our feelings as well. In developing values we become aware of what we prize and cherish. Our feelings help us determine what we think is worthy and important, what our priorities are.

5. *Publicly affirming.*

When we share our choices with others—what we prize and what we do—we not only continue to clarify our own values, but we help others to clarify their values as well. It is important to encourage students to speak out about their beliefs and their actions in appropriate ways and circumstances.

ACTING on one's beliefs

6. *Acting.*

Often people have difficulty in acting on what

33

they come to believe and prize. Yet, if they are to realize their values, it is vital that they learn how to connect choices and prizings to their own behavior.

7. *Acting with some pattern.*

A single act does not make a value. We need to examine the patterns of our lives. What do we do with consistency and regularity? Do these patterns incorporate our choices and prizings? If our life patterns do not reflect our choices and prizings, we then must reconsider our priorities or change our behavior in order to actualize those priorities.

Collectively, these seven subprocesses comprise the total valuing process. Students who have built the process of choosing, prizing, and acting into their lives have learned an approach to living which is uniquely their own. The process will serve them effectively as they are confronted with controversial issues, values choices, and life dilemmas.

Ideally, teaching extends beyond the facts level and the concepts level to include this valuing process at the third level—the values level.

GUIDELINES FOR VALUES-LEVEL TEACHING

Values-level questions and activities are aimed at fostering the valuing process. For values-level teaching to be successful, there are guidelines built into the teacher's role.

The teacher who instructs at the values level is accepting and nonjudgmental. He may correct students

34

on the facts level, but he understands there are no right and wrong answers to questions at the values level. He may offer his own viewpoint, but he is careful to describe it as his opinion, not as the final answer. A teacher may preface his views with a statement such as: "That's an interesting viewpoint. These are my ideas. Does anyone else have a different viewpoint or want to react to one already stated?" He gives his opinion without monopolizing the discussion, then moves on to other opinions.

Unfortunately, teachers frequently sound most authoritative when discussing values issues. Too often they adamantly defend their position as the only tenable one. Teachers who avoid an authoritative attitude find that students are able to respond honestly.

The open and nonjudgmental teacher will provide an atmosphere that encourages diversity. Since students are accustomed to viewing the teacher as an authority, they may be predisposed to a teacher's position. The teacher must reassure his students that they will not be censured for expressing an opinion that differs from his.

Respect for the individual's right to pass is essential to the values-clarification process. When working on the values level, each person has the right to participate or not, to answer or not. The teacher emphasizes this right, especially when initiating the values approach. The right to pass not only protects the student's privacy, but also safeguards the teacher from critics who believe he has no right to ask students personal, values questions.

Just as a teacher using the values approach respects the individual's right to pass, *he must also respect the student's response* without commenting on or probing into the individual's reasons unnecessarily. Teachers can legitimately raise a question or two about the reasons for a student's choice. However, since the purpose of a values question is to help individuals clarify and affirm their own values, he will not want to defeat that purpose by putting students on the defensive. Students who feel criticized, threatened, or attacked will become closed to new thinking.

Students who choose to participate should be encouraged to respond honestly. Many students with problems in values development try to reflect the adult or peer group's point of view rather than search for their own. When the teacher senses this, *he asks values-clarifying questions:* "What are your real feelings?" "Are there some other alternatives?" "What are the consequences of your decision?" It helps to frequently ask "you" questions—questions which ask about the students' own ideas, actions, and intentions. Clarifying questions will encourage students to evaluate alternatives and consequences. But to raise clarifying questions, a teacher must hear what the students actually say. Although listening is sometimes difficult in a classroom, *the teacher should be a model of good listening for the students.*

When controversial issues or values choices are discussed, *some questions are to be avoided.* For example,

*This topic is explored more fully in *Values and Teaching* (30).

36

questions that demand a "yes-no" or an "either-or" answer limit thinking. "Why" questions, while sometimes justified, risk pushing students who have no clear reasons for their choices into fabricating a reason. Rather than asking "Why?" a teacher asks: "Do you have a reason?" Similarly, instead of asking "What other alternatives did you consider?" he asks, "Have you considered any other alternatives?"

As the teacher raises values questions over a period of time, *he includes questions that relate to social issues as well as individual concerns.* "You" questions can too easily involve only personal concerns—family, money, friends. Today, students need to consider broader social, national, and international issues such as war, race, ecology, poverty. Again, the teacher encourages diversity, even by playing the role of devil's advocate. It is easy for teachers to avoid controversial issues or to encourage comments on only one side of an issue. But students need to examine the alternatives of an issue without settling for simplistic thinking or inadequate communication.

Values-clarification is effective when a teacher:

- is accepting and nonjudgmental.

- encourages diversity; realizes that there are no absolute right or wrong answers for another's values questions.

- respects the individual's choice to participate or not.

- respects the individual's response.

- encourages each person to answer honestly.

- listens and raises clarifying questions with students.

- avoids questions which may threaten or limit thinking.

- raises questions of both personal and social concern.

These guidelines help the teacher engage students in the valuing process—the goal of values-clarification.

Examples From the Different Subject Areas

Before considering examples of three-level teaching in the various subject areas, it might be useful to respond to a question which teachers often ask:

How can you always be sure which of the three teaching levels is being used? For example, if a class were asked to memorize three ways that Newton's laws affect their own lives, would that be teaching on the facts or the concepts or the values level?

It's true that the distinction between the *content* of the subject and the *method* by which it is taught often makes it difficult to identify which of the three levels of teaching is being employed. In the final analysis, the critical distinction between the three levels of teaching is *how the student subjectively apprehends the material.* No matter how a student is taught, whether by rote, inductively, or creatively, if he feels he's learned an isolated piece of information—even one as important as the formula $E=mc^2$—then, for him, learning is taking place on the facts level. But if he sees a connection between the formula and its function, or feels he understands what he has learned in a more insightful or experiential way, then he is learning on the concepts level. To memorize the relativity equation is to learn a fact. To grasp its meaning, even in the most tentative way, is to gain a concept. And, finally, when the learner can subjectively make the connection between the subject matter and his own life, when the subject matter helps him engage in one or more of the seven valuing subprocesses, then the values level has been reached.

If the ultimate distinction between the three levels takes place within the student, the level of teaching is judged by the level of learning. Thus, teaching which results in the student learning isolated data is facts-level teaching; teaching which results in the student understanding an abstraction, a relationship, or a complicated skill process is concepts-level teaching; and teaching which results in the student relating the subject matter to his own life through the valuing processes (prizing, choosing, and acting) is values-level teaching.

At this point, perhaps, many readers are thinking: "I see the possibility of three-level teaching when you talk about the Pilgrim story. But I teach mathematics! How am I supposed to teach that on the values level? And what about vocabulary...or science...or music...or all the other subjects in the curriculum?"

41

In this chapter, there are examples of values-level teaching in a wide variety of subject areas.*†These areas are:

Literature	**Physics**
Vocabulary	**Foreign Languages**
Grammar	**Home Economics**
Civics	**Physical Education**
History	**Health**
Social Studies	**Art**
Mathematics	**Music**
Earth Science	**Religion**
Biology	**Bookkeeping**
Chemistry	**Typing & Shorthand**

*The authors realize that many of these subject area distinctions are arbitrary and many schools no longer use them. However, since most schools still do use them, they provide a convenient format for presenting the following examples.

†Many of the examples in this chapter are excerpted or adapted from articles the authors have written in various journals. The articles are listed in the bibliography. All excerpts are used with permission of the publishers.

The intention of this chapter is not to prescribe a curriculum in each subject. A few examples can hardly do justice to any subject area. But perhaps the examples will suggest a direction in which teachers in various disciplines may go. The reader need not feel bound to read this entire chapter, but rather, may wish to concentrate on his own subject area and others which interest him.

LITERATURE

Poetry

The Road Not Taken

Two roads diverged in a yellow wood,
And sorry I could not travel both
And be one traveler, long I stood
And looked down one as far as I could
To where it bent in the undergrowth;

Then took the other, as just as fair,
And having perhaps the better claim,
Because it was grassy and wanted wear;
Though as for that, the passing there
Had worn them really about the same,

And both that morning equally lay
In leaves no step had trodden black.
Oh, I kept the first for another day!
Yet knowing how way leads on to way,
I doubted if I should ever come back.

I shall be telling this with a sigh
Somewhere ages and ages hence:
Two roads diverged in a wood, and I—
I took the one less traveled by,
And that has made all the difference.

Robert Frost

44

FACTS LEVEL

1. Memorize the poem.

2. Who was the author?

3. When was the poem written?

4. What was the background of the writer?

5. What is its rhythmic pattern?

CONCEPTS LEVEL

1. What is the poet saying in this poem? What do you think the two roads mean?

2. In what school of poetry would you place Robert Frost? Discuss.

3. How would you compare Frost's style of verse to that of e.e. cummings?

4. How does Frost relate to his New England heritage and men like Emerson, Thoreau, and Longfellow? What concepts do they have in common?

VALUES LEVEL

1. Write a poem on how you feel about making decisions. What images can you use other than a road?

2. What was the most important choice you had to make in your life?

3. Have you ever faced a "grassy" road that "wanted wear"?

4. In what way(s) has one of your choices made a difference in your life?

5. Which of your choices are you most proud of? Do you have reasons?

6. Is there any adult who gives you helpful advice when you face choices?

7. Are you at or are you coming to any new forks in the road? How do you think you'll choose? What are the pros and cons of the alternatives?

The poem and questions above could be used as a Values Sheet, which usually takes the form of a provocative quotation with questions that relate the quotation to the students' lives. If the Values Sheet is duplicated, each student has the opportunity to answer the questions. Their responses can be shared with other students or the teacher. Values Sheets can also be used as the basis for small group discussions.

Almost any piece of literature can be used similarly to stimulate students to think about values questions.

VOCABULARY

FACTS LEVEL

1. Memorize the meaning of the following words:

commitment	inferiority	touch
fascination	reliable	arduous

2. Tell whether each word is a noun, verb, or adjective.

CONCEPTS LEVEL

1. Use each of the above words in a sentence.

2. Define each of them in your own words.

3. Change the form of each of the words.

VALUES LEVEL

1. Make up sentences out of your own life that use some of these words. The sentences should tell something about who you are or what you value.

2. Fill in one of the following incomplete sentences and use one or two of the above words.

> I like.... I feel.... I wonder.... I thought....
> I don't like.... I don't want.... I wish that....

Responses on the values level can be shared as the class reviews their vocabulary words.

GRAMMAR

Punctuation

This section illustrates a method of combining a study of punctuation with a sharing of student activities, thoughts, and feelings. Such sharing helps students become aware of themselves and others and aids them in making choices.

1. First, students are asked to work alone, completing sentences and punctuating them properly. Here are some sentence stems to work with:

    a. Three television programs I like are....

    b. On Saturday I love to....

    c. If I had a hundred dollars I would....

    d. I'd like to say to my father....

2. Then, students might write their sentences on the chalkboard and answer questions about the punctuation and questions from the class referring to the meaning. Alternatively, students might do this in groups of three or four, perhaps with each group selecting an example of punctuation used both properly and improperly to show the whole class.

48

CIVICS

The Constitution

FACTS LEVEL

1. In what order did the states ratify the Constitution?

2. What were the major differences between the Constitution and the Articles of Confederation? (This would be a concepts-level question if the students discovered the differences for themselves, instead of memorizing the teacher's answer to this question.)

3. Name the founding fathers who were most instrumental in the formation of the Constitution and tell the part that each played.

4. What powers does the Constitution give to each branch of government?

5. What did the Constitution originally state on the issue of slavery?

6. Describe the ten amendments which make up the Bill of Rights?

CONCEPTS LEVEL

1. What are some current civil liberties issues that relate to the Bill of Rights?

2. What were the causes of the American Revolution, and how typical were they of revolutions in general?

3. Compare our system of separation of powers to a parliamentary system like England's. What are the advantages and disadvantages of each? Compare our system to that of a dictatorship. What are the advantages and disadvantages of each?

4. If the Constitution had declared slavery illegal, how might the course of American history have been different?

5. What was the reasoning behind separating the powers into three branches of government?

VALUES LEVEL

1. If you were at the Constitutional Convention, how would you have voted on the questions of slavery? What have students your age done about the race problem in America today? If you care about that problem, have you done anything to help?

2. Compare the ways in which decisions are made in the United States government with the ways decisions are made in your family. Are there checks and balances in your family? What part do you play in family decisions?

3. If you wanted to change something in our society or in this school, what are some ways you would go about it? Have you ever tried any of these ways?

4. The First Amendment affirms the right of freedom of speech. Have you recently made use of that freedom in a way you are proud of?

5. Here are five civil liberties issues which have recently come up before the Supreme Court. Before I tell you the Court's decisions, I would like you to divide into committees and pretend that you are the Supreme Court. How would you decide on each? Give your reasons.

Almost any topic in a civics course is a values topic. Students also have opportunities to involve themselves directly in local politics. They can relate their views to elected representatives and can work on many community issues.

HISTORY

The Civil War

FACTS LEVEL

1. What were the provisions of the Emancipation Proclamation? When was it made?

2. Who was Robert E. Lee?

3. What happened at Fort Sumter?

4. How did Lincoln's position shift during the period of the war?

5. List five major battles of the war in the order of their occurrence.

CONCEPTS LEVEL

1. To what extent did the war serve useful purposes? Compare the purposes of this war with those of other wars.

2. Who does your history book imply are the heroes and villains in the war? What qualities or events make a hero or a villain?

3. Discuss the role of inspirational leaders in the Civil War and the role, generally, of inspirational leaders in society.

4. Compare the Civil War with current struggles in America. What similarities and differences do you find?

5. Might the Civil War have been prevented? What principles of preventing war can you suggest that might be applicable in the United States and the world today?

VALUES LEVEL

1. Do you consider the Civil War a just war? If you had been there to choose, on which side would you have fought, if any?

2. What would have been your reaction if you were drafted to fight on one side but did not sympathize entirely with that side? If this happened to you in the future, what would you do?

3. Under what circumstances would you kill a person?

4. What kinds of living things would you kill without concern?

5. How are disputes settled in your family? What can you do to experiment with better ways of settling disputes?

6. Have you ever acted—written a letter to an editor or congressman or tried to influence someone else's thinking—to help prevent a war or other conflict? What *can* persons your age do?

7. How do you react to inspirational leaders? Might you follow such a leader down roads you disapprove of?

8. What is your position on some of the civil disputes raging in our country today? Have you done anything to reduce the potential for violence in any of them?

Almost any unit in history can be handled readily on all three levels.

SOCIAL STUDIES

Minority Groups or Poverty

FACTS LEVEL

1. How many blacks are there in the United States?

2. Where do most of them live?

3. What is a ghetto?

4. How many Indians and Spanish-speaking people do we have in this country?

5. Where do most of these people live?

6. What is the government policy concerning Indians on reservations?

7. What is the percentage of unemployed among minority groups?

CONCEPTS LEVEL

1. What are the goals of the civil rights movement? How have they evolved?

2. Why do blacks have a higher unemployment rate and lower average incomes than whites with comparable education?

3. Contrast the situation of blacks and Spanish-speaking people today with that of earlier immigrant groups. What are the similarities and differences?

4. What are some reasons for the plight of the American Indian?

VALUES LEVEL

1. Do you think that government policy should favor assimilation of Indians into society, self-determination of each tribe, or some other alternative? Explain your position. Would you be willing to inform the Secretary of the Interior of your views?

2. Below are some activities or projects designed to sensitize students to aspects of reality. Members of the class might choose experiences they would like to have, designating first, second, and third choices. Then the class could be divided into small groups to make arrangements for their experiences. Be sure to allow time for students to discuss their experiences, vent their feelings, and discuss any changes in their opinions or values.

• Visit the local welfare agency. Interview a social worker to determine some of the reasons people apply for public assistance.

• Ask a middle-class black student in your school about the places in which he or she has lived. Find out what experiences his or her family has had with real estate agents.

• Go to one of the small grocery stores in a ghetto neighborhood a week before welfare checks come out and note the prices on various staples. Go back the day checks come out and see if there are any price changes.

• Attend church services some Sunday in a store-front church.

• Go to a magistrate's court and keep a list of the kinds of cases brought before the magistrate. Who are the clients? How are they handled?

• Visit a free clinic in a low-income neighborhood. Strike up a conversation with a patient in the waiting room.

• Visit an area into which blacks are just moving. Survey the names of the real estate companies who have signs posted. Try to find out if they have been involved in blockbusting in the city.

• Visit an Indian tribe or agencies for Indians in your area. If you visit an agency, interview the people about the availability of jobs and housing. If you visit a tribe, talk with one of the members about his Indian heritage.

• Visit a store in a Spanish- or Oriental-speaking neighborhood. Find out what foods customers like best and ask one to give you a favorite recipe. Try out the food.

3. Whom would you like as your neighbor? Rank your preferences from most desirable to least desirable. This is all you know about them.

        a. an Indian family
        b. a white family
        c. a Negro family
        d. a Puerto Rican family

4. Explain to what extent you are a racist.

5. At one extreme we have Super Separatist Sam, whose solution to the race problem is to ship every human being back to his original country. He advocates imprisoning people whose ancestors came from two different countries. At the other extreme we find Multi-Mixing Mike, who insists that all babies be distributed to couples of another race. In addition, he insists that no couples of the same race marry and that couples of the same race already married must be divorced and marry outside their race. Between these extremes, where would you place yourself, nearer Super Separatist Sam or nearer Multi-Mixing Mike? Explain your position.

Super
Separatist
Sam

Multi-
Mixing
Mike

58

6. Respond to the man who says this: "I have no prejudices against Negroes. I simply believe that we need to take a long-range view of this problem. Most need to have more education. When they are ready, then I think they will get jobs just like anyone else."

7. Would you write a letter to your congressman or senator which expresses your views on civil rights? Explain. Would you organize a petition or take part in a peaceful demonstration for civil rights? Explain. Would you engage in violent protest? Explain.

Most units or topics in social studies can be taught on all three levels. As with civics, there is frequently the opportunity for students to engage in community projects.

MATHEMATICS

This section indicates how some mathematics lessons can be extended to the values level. This can be done on occasion to vary the tone of math classes and to exercise student valuing skills.

Problem: Bill bought a three-speed bike for thirty-five dollars. Three years later, he sold it for fifteen dollars. While he owned the bike, he spent nine dollars on repairs. How much did it cost Bill to use his bike each year? What percent of the purchase price did he lose when he sold it?

VALUES LEVEL

1. Under what conditions would you tell a buyer what was wrong with something you were trying to sell him? What if he didn't ask?

2. Would you lower the price to someone who was poor?

3. If you didn't sell your old playthings, what else might you do with them?

Problem: June works one hour a week washing the kitchen floor for her mother. She also spends fifteen minutes every evening drying dishes. It takes her about thirty minutes a week to straighten her room. How much time does June spend working around the house each week? Each year? What proportion of her work time does she spend drying dishes?

VALUES LEVEL

1. Do you think that June should be paid for her housework? For all of it, part of it, or none of it? Do you get paid for doing chores around the house?

2. If she is paid for her housework, then do you think June should help pay for her food and clothing? What do you pay for out of your allowance?

3. If you ever have children, how will you handle chores around the house?

4. What can you do now to improve the way work is done around your house? What are your chores? How do you feel about doing them? Is it easy or hard for you?

Problem: For the bottled drinks listed below, determine which is the best buy for your money.

Coca-Cola:	*Price:*
12-oz. deposit bottles	8 for $1.05 (plus 5¢ per bottle)
26-oz. deposit bottles	1 for 19¢ (plus 15¢ per bottle)
12-oz. pop-top cans	6 for 95¢

Pepsi Cola:	*Price:*
26-oz. no-deposit bottles	1 for 34¢
12-oz. pop-top cans	6 for 95¢
12-oz. deposit bottles	8 for $1.05 (plus 5¢ per bottle)

VALUES LEVEL

1. In answering the following questions, raise your hand if you agree (wave it if you strongly agree), cross your arms if you aren't sure or don't want to say, and put your thumb down if you disagree (move your thumb up and down if you strongly disagree).

- How many of you like coke?

- How many of you like milk?

- How many of you drink at least three cans of soda pop a day?

- How many of you spend over a dollar of your own money on soda pop each week?

- How many of you buy mainly bottles that require no deposit?

- How many of you often ask to have soda pop rather than milk at meals?

2. How many of you receive a weekly allowance? What do you spend most of your money on? Are you proud of this?

3. How many of you try to save money? What are you saving your money for? Is this your choice?

62

4. What influences what you buy? Rank the following in order of importance.

a. the price
b. advertising
c. your parents
d. your friends

5. If there were a campaign to collect coke bottles for recycling, would you participate? Would you start such a campaign?

Project: Have the students keep a record of how they spend their money. Then work out problems and values questions based on that record. For example: What percentage of your expenditures goes toward purchases that last only a short time, like a soda or a movie ticket? What percentage goes toward purchases that last a long time, like a baseball or a record? What fraction of your income required work? Would you want your life's work to be any more enjoyable than this work?

Project: Have the students keep a time diary—a chart which shows how they spend all their time, each day. Then work out problems and values questions based on their own statistics. Here are some examples, with values questions in parentheses.
1. What percentage of your waking hours is spent with others? What percentage is spent alone? (Do you like this balance? Is it right for you? For everyone? Why do some people always need people around them? In what

ways do you spend time differently from others your age?)

2. Using the total time you slept last week as an average, how many hours per year do you sleep? What is the ratio of your sleeping time to the time you spend in nonschool activities? (Do you get enough sleep to satisfy you? What activities might you eliminate if you wanted more time to sleep? What is the best time of day for you to do difficult things? How does not getting enough sleep affect your behavior?)

3. On the average, how much free time a day do you have? What percentage of this time is spent watching TV? (How do you handle conflicts with other members of your family over what to watch? The last time your television wasn't working, what did you do with your free time?)

Project: Take a poll of students' attitudes toward several things that you or they think are important. Then put your findings in graph form. Discuss your reasons for selecting those items to survey. Then analyze and discuss the data on the graph.

Project: Have students work with an imaginary budget of a million dollars to improve their school. Then ask: how would you spend it? Be specific. Obtain facts from the principal, business office, and so forth. Keep in mind that how you spend money usually indicates what you value.

Project: Have students estimate the number of hours

64

the light(s) in their room burns each week. Have them calculate the number of kilowatt hours used. Then have them calculate the cost per hour when the light in their room is on. (Careful. Don't moralize. Now that they know the consequences of leaving their lights on, ask them: How many of you will leave your light on more often now when you leave your room? How many will leave your light on less often? How many will leave it on about as often as before?)

EARTH SCIENCE

The Earth's Crust

FACTS LEVEL

1. What are the major groups of rocks?

2. How are rocks formed?

3. Which group of rocks is the oldest? When was it formed?

4. What are three ways water can change the earth's surface?

5. What precious gems are found among the minerals in the earth?

6. How are volcanoes formed?

CONCEPTS LEVEL

1. Show how two recent dramatic changes of the earth's surface were similar to changes which took place a million years ago.

2. Compare and contrast two theories of how mountains were formed. Which do you accept? Give your reasons.

3. Discuss the similarities and differences between precious and semiprecious stones.

4. Where on the earth's surface are volcanoes most likely to occur today? Why?

5. Demonstrate your knowledge of rocks or minerals by collecting and labeling various samples.

VALUES LEVEL

1. Are you someone who is likely to become a rock collector?

2. Are the mountains a place where you really like to spend your vacations? Where would you like to go on vacation? What do you like to do best on vacation?

3. Should oil companies receive a depletion allowance? Give reasons for your answer.

4. In some states strip miners find it cheaper to pay the fine than to do the reforestation the law requires. What is your reaction to this? What other information do you feel you need to know about this?

5. Which, if any, of these worry you? Rank them with the least desirable appearing first.

• Converting the Florida Everglades into a jetport for Miami.

• Bulldozing through a mountain range to construct a four-lane road.

• Spreading cities over the earth's surface, leaving less and less open space.

• Turning a wildlife preserve into an amusement park.

6. As you know, much of our jewelry comes from rocks and stones. If you get married, do you think you will give an expensive ring to your wife? Or, if you are a girl, do you think you will want one? Can you think of any other ways a husband might show his affection for his bride?

7. It is too hard for a city to maintain grass in public places; all the ground should be asphalt. Do you agree or disagree? Give your reasons.

8. How do you think you would have answered these questions last year? Describe how your answers have changed, if they have.

There are other areas in earth and space science where all three levels might be taught. For example: weather, electricity, consumer questions such as use of phosphates, fluoridation of water supplies, scientific method, pollution of air and water, and space exploration.

68

BIOLOGY

The Study and Dissection of a Frog

FACTS LEVEL

1. To what species, class, and family do frogs belong? What characteristics distinguish the class and family? Name some other members of the class.

2. Name and identify the parts of the frog's body.

3. How do frogs reproduce?

4. What are a frog's stages of development?

5. What do frogs eat?

CONCEPTS LEVEL

1. How do frogs contribute to the balance of nature?

2. What are the similarities and differences between the development of the frog and the development of the human infant?

3. What physiological processes in the frog are present in all animal life?

4. Build a terrarium for frogs. From your observations, what are the characteristics of the frog's social behavior?

69

5. In dissecting a frog, the pancreas and mesentery are removed. What would happen to you if yours were removed?

VALUES LEVEL

1. Which would you rather dissect? (Rank in order from first to last choice.)

> a. a frog
> b. a rat
> c. a worm
> d. a pig

What are the reasons for your choice?

2. Would you consider willing an eye or kidney to the eye or kidney bank? Would you donate your body to science?

3. Would you eat a frog? Have you ever eaten one? If you were lost in the woods and were starving, where would you draw the line about what you would or would not eat? Would you eat worms, mice, any mushrooms? If a war came and you were starving, where would you draw the line about what animals you would eat?

4. Parsi Paul believes that all life is sacred and no one should kill any living creature. He eats no meat, will not swat a mosquito, and even steps around a cock-

roach. Experimental Elbert believes that the only way science can move ahead is to experiment on all living things, including people, even if it means death. Where would you place yourself on the line between these two extremes, closer to Parsi Paul or Experimental Elbert? How do you feel about the killing of animals for man's purposes?

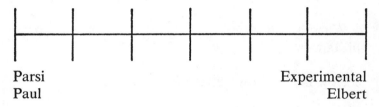

Parsi   Experimental
Paul   Elbert

Other biology topics very easily taken to the values level are ecology, sex, diet and digestion, care of the body, genetics, and intelligence.

CHEMISTRY

The Periodic Table

FACTS LEVEL

1. What is the valence of hydrogen, potassium, and oxygen?

2. What is the atomic weight of each of the above substances?

3. How many known elements are there?

4. What elements are inert?

5. What are the special characteristics of C?

6. Define an atom and a molecule.

7. What is the special characteristic of radium?

8. What does + or - valence mean for an element?

CONCEPTS LEVEL

1. What is the relationship between + and - valences?

2. Why are certain elements inert?

3. How did the discovery of radium relate to atomic energy?

72

4. How does the special characteristic of C relate to organic matter?

5. What generalizations can you make about elements when you look at the periodic table?

6. From looking at the periodic table, what assumptions can you make about the universe?

VALUES LEVEL

1. Fill in the following open-ended sentences:

• I think a knowledge of chemistry has helped mankind because....

• I think man has misused his chemical knowledge because....

2. Which of the following projects do you believe to be most important? Rank all three in the order of your priorities.

• Creating a new agent to protect crops from disease.

• Determining a way to take mercury from our lakes and rivers.

• Researching a cure for cancer.

3. How do you feel about the development of atomic weapons? Have you written your views to your congressman or to the daily newspaper? What are your

reasons for thinking that we should or should not have dropped an atom bomb on Hiroshima?

4. What can a person your age do about air or water pollution?

5. Under what conditions would you take a job in a defense industry which produces chemical warfare agents? What are the reasons for your decision?

6. Hold a debate in class on the question of whether chemists should be interested only in discovering the truth without regard for how their discoveries are used in society. Should chemists be involved in determining government policies on the use of their discoveries?

Other values topics could be: use of scientific discoveries; what drugs, alcohol, and cigarettes do to the body; study of the public health hazards of poor garbage disposal or of certain chemicals such as mercury; the drug industry, the high costs of drugs, and the danger of new drugs.

PHYSICS

Newton's Laws

FACTS LEVEL

1. What are Newton's laws? What are the formulae derived from the laws?

2. When were the laws formulated?

3. Which is called the "first law"?

4. What laws did Newton's laws make obsolete?

CONCEPTS LEVEL

1. Demonstrate, through laboratory experiments, that you know these laws.

2. How are these principles used in recent inventions?

3. Attempt to invent something useful by applying one or more of Newton's laws.

4. Describe the applications of these laws in the machines used in moon shots.

VALUES LEVEL

1. How, if at all, have these laws touched your own life?

2. Seat belts in cars are related to one of these laws. Do you have them in the car in which you drive most often? Do you use them? Explain.

3. What's the fastest you have ever driven a car? If you aren't the driver, at what speed would you insist that the driver slow down?

4. What is your position on the following statement? Scientists and inventors have an obligation to see that their discoveries, like the automobile, are not used to hurt man.

5. One of Newton's laws says, "Every action has an equal and opposite reaction." Can you apply this principle to your relationship with other people? Does this suggest anything different you want to do in your life?

FOREIGN LANGUAGES

Literature selections read in a foreign language could be taken to the third level simply by asking a few questions in the language or in English, if necessary, that connect the meaning of the literature to the choices, prizings, or actions of the students. See the section on literature for some examples.

Look also at the values-level teaching examples in the section on English for ideas adaptable to foreign-language teaching. In some cases, mixed languages might be used. For example, a group of beginning Spanish students might complete these values-oriented sentences, using as much Spanish as they can.

• Con cien dolares, I would....
(With a hundred dollars, I would....)

• En los sabados, I love to....
(On Saturdays, I love to....)

• I would like to tell mi amigo....
(I would like to tell my friend....)

• The President debe....
(The President ought to....)

Almost any of the values strategies can be used in this mixed language format or, for more advanced students, entirely in the foreign language. One could ask beginning French students "values voting" questions:

- Combien de vous aimez to watch television?
(How many of you like to watch television?)

- Combien de vous ont des amis d'autre race or religion?
(How many of you have friends of another race or religion?)

- Combien de vous believe que la guerre au Vietnam was a mistake?
(How many believe that the Vietnam war was a mistake?)

See the books *Values and Teaching* (30) and *Values Clarification: A Handbook of Practical Strategies* (37) for many more classroom strategies adaptable for foreign languages.

HOME ECONOMICS

Foods

FACTS LEVEL

1. What foods are needed daily for a balanced diet?

2. What vitamins do you find in the following vegetables: carrots, spinach, green peas, tomatoes?

3. What is the average adult daily requirement of fat and carbohydrates? What is the daily requirement for a ten-year-old child?

4. What happens to children if they have a deficiency of vitamin C, B, or K?

5. How many people in the world go to bed hungry? How many in the United States suffer from malnutrition?

CONCEPTS LEVEL

1. Plan a week of balanced meals for a family of four. Indicate the cost of each meal.

2. The average food allowance for a person on welfare recently was seventy-five cents per day in states where grants are high. Plan a week of balanced meals for two adults and two children on welfare. What difficulties did you encounter?

3. How are the personality and abilities of a person affected by an inadequate diet?

4. Why do hunger and starvation exist even though we have the technical knowledge to alleviate them?

5. How is overpopulation related to the problem of hunger and inadequate medical care?

6. What problems do consumers encounter in buying foods?

VALUES LEVEL

1. Ask your family to live on your state's weekly welfare budget for food. Then discuss what the experience meant to you.

2. What is your favorite dinner? What happens in your family if one of you doesn't like something that's being served?

3. Have you ever done anything about consumer practices? What did you do?

4. In this voting exercise, raise your hand if you agree (wave if you agree passionately), fold your arms if you're not sure how you feel or don't want to say, and put your thumb down if you disagree (move it up and down if you disagree strongly).

• How many of you like steak?

- How many of you eat in a restaurant once a week?

- How many of you have ever gone on a diet?

- How many of you drink at least one coke per day?

- How many of you drink at least two glasses of milk per day?

- How many of you eat junk between meals?

- How many of you often go without breakfast?

- How many of you eat fresh fruit once a day?

- How many of you wish there was more food to eat at mealtimes?

5. Name something that you cooked which you are proud of.

6. Would you want to feed a future family of yours the foods you generally eat? What would be similar or different?

Other areas in home economics which concern all three levels of instruction are: use of money; fair consumer practices; child-rearing; roles of men and women; hunger in America and the world; home and health practices of various cultures; choosing and furnishing a home.

PHYSICAL EDUCATION

Students may wish to participate in occasional large or small group discussions where values issues can be raised. Or the physical education teacher, speaking briefly to a student in passing, may ask values questions such as these:

1. To a boy or girl who is sad at having lost in competition: What is the hardest thing about losing for you? How does it make you feel?

2. To a hard worker: You seem to be working hard at improving your skills. Do you usually work hard at things?

3. To a student who took initiative: Do you usually take initiative as you did today? How does that help others? Does it ever cause any problems for others?

4. To someone who has urged his colleagues to work cooperatively: Have you thought through the possible disadvantages teamwork might have?

The following topics and questions could be raised with an entire class:

1. Is there enough physical exercise in your life? Too much? What might you do to improve your physical condition? Make a list and try to do one or two things you listed.

2. It's often said that a healthy body serves a healthy mind. How true has this been for you?

3. What are some ways people can feel the way they want to without drinking alcoholic beverages? Make a list of ways. Which ones are less harmful than alcohol? (Can also be used with smoking and drug abuse.)

4. What are the best sports to play? To watch? See if your group can agree.

5. Think of something you did to overcome a fear. Would volunteers share their thoughts?

6. In what ways are you self-disciplined? When do you need outside motivation in order to do your work? Discuss.

7. List reasons why sports give you pleasure. What on your list do you feel best (second best, etc.) about?

8. How do you make choices about what to do with your free time?

9. In sports, there are some people who often feel left out or inadequate. What are some helpful things that might be done for such persons? What would not be helpful?

10. How could our physical education program be made more satisfying to more students? How can we work at implementing some of these improvements?

11. Other than sports, what are some ways to get healthy bodies? Which have you tried? Which have been pleasurable?

12. Rank the following in terms of importance to you: strength, agility, endurance, grace, coordination. Which abilities are you actively trying to improve, if any?

HEALTH

Sex Education and Family Living

FACTS LEVEL

1. How does pregnancy take place in a woman?

2. What is the function of the menstrual cycle?

3. What happens when the egg and sperm unite?

4. How long does it take for a human embryo to develop? Describe the stages of development.

5. Define the following words: chromosome, gene, ovum, semen, uterus.

CONCEPTS LEVEL

1. What are the similarities between human reproduction and animal reproduction?

2. How does sexuality relate to love?

3. What is the function of the family in facilitating the growth of a human infant?

4. What child-rearing practices exist in America? Do these differ from the past? Are there differences between classes and cultures?

5. What generalizations can we make about the roles of men and women in our society?

VALUES LEVEL

1. Finish the following sentence and then explain the reasons for your views in a few more sentences.

- I think Women's Liberation is....

2. Rank the following items according to your first, second, and third choice.

Mothers should:

- Stay at home with their children, including teenagers.
- Work at a full-time job if they choose to.
- Participate in community organizations.

Fathers should:

- Be able to come home after work and just relax.
- Help around the house with dishes and the cleaning.
- Only help with chores like repairs and cutting grass.

Fathers should:

- Be willing to listen to their children's ideas.
- Take each child on an outing of the child's choice.
- Let their children do as they please.

86

Mothers should:

- Referee children's fights, but not play favorites.
- Be in charge of all discipline of the children.
- Allow children to work out disputes by themselves.

3. Make a montage of magazine pictures expressing your feelings and thoughts on what makes a man (boy) or a woman (girl).

4. Ask the class to vote on the following questions (seventh grade examples). They might raise their hands if they agree (wave it if they agree strongly), fold their arms if they don't know or don't want to say, and put thumbs down if they disagree (move thumb up and down if they strongly disagree).

- How many of you think girls should never telephone boys?

- How many of you think that going steady is OK?

- How many of you would rather have girls and boys in separate classes?

- How many of you like to dance?

- How many of you think kissing is OK?

- How many of you think kissing is better than television?

• How many of you would like to go out on more dates?

5. How do you decide what to do and what not to do on dates? Do your guidelines work for you? Is there anyone who helps you with problems of love, sex, and dating?

Other values areas in health might be: problems of drugs, alcohol, smoking; recreation and fun; sleep and eating habits; family patterns and problems; feelings about the body.

ART

Painting

FACTS LEVEL

1. Stretch a canvas.

2. Demonstrate how to use a palette knife.

3. Name three warm colors.

4. What is a landscape?

CONCEPTS LEVEL

1. What is the function of perspective? How is perspective created?

2. Try to paint the still life you see before you.

3. Demonstrate how light and shadow are used in painting.

VALUES LEVEL

1. What would you like to paint, if you could? What would you most like to communicate through painting?

2. What are your favorite colors?

3. Which would you rather paint? Rank the following

from most desirable to least desirable. Then share the reasons for your order.

    a. a portrait
    b. an abstract
    c. a still life
    d. a figure
    e. a landscape

4. Create a still life from objects you feel represent either the best in our culture or the worst in our culture.

5. Using water colors, quickly create a painting that communicates the emotion you are feeling most strongly right now. Tell how you felt about the process and how you feel about the product.

6. When you have completed a painting, do you want others to see it? What does that do for you?

Art Appreciation

FACTS LEVEL

1. What kinds of columns are found on the Parthenon?

2. Who sculpted *The Thinker?*

3. Name three Impressionist painters.

4. Define pointillism.

5. What is a line drawing?

90

CONCEPTS LEVEL

1. Compare the architecture of the Notre Dame cathedral with the cathedral at Chartres.

2. Discuss how space is used in sculpture.

3. Compare three different paintings of Christ.

4. How has art been used as effective protest? Bring in examples.

VALUES LEVEL

1. Choose an artist whose work you particularly like. Share your feelings about the artist's work.

2. If you could talk to Picasso, what would you say to him?

3. What part, if any, does art now play in your life? How would your life be different without art?

4. Would you like to have your surroundings more artistic? What is one thing you could do to achieve that? Will you do it?

5. What kinds of museums, if any, do you like? Could you design a museum that you would like better than those you now know?

6. How do you go about looking at art works? What do you do first, second, last? Have you experimented to see if there is something else you might do to get more satisfaction out of art?

7. Do you like to view art with others or by yourself? If others are involved, what do they do that helps you enjoy art? What detracts from your enjoyment?

8. Most artists in our society have a difficult financial struggle. Do you think this should be changed? List some things that might be done to change this situation. Would you be willing to try to help bring about one of these changes?

9. Look at this work of art. What does it say to you? How does it make you feel? ("What was the artist trying to express?" would be a concepts-level question.)

10. Here are several works of art. Rank the different works in order, from the one you like best to the one you like least. Explain any reasons you have for your ranking. Can you think of any music or literature that expresses the feelings you get from any of these works of art?

11. Rank the following in order from most artistic to least artistic.

> a. your bedroom
> b. your living room
> c. this classroom

a. a new automobile
b. an old automobile in good condition
c. a motorcycle

Art teachers may get other ideas by looking at the following section on Music.

MUSIC

Instrumental Training

FACTS LEVEL

1. Demonstrate how to hold the musical instrument.

2. Name the different parts of the instrument.

3. Demonstrate the fingering of a C-major scale.

4. Show how to slur, bar, mute, flutter, etc. (depending on the instrument).

5. What is a time signature? An octave? A treble clef?

6. What do the following terms mean: allegro, crescendo, adagio, forte, pizzicato?

CONCEPTS LEVEL

1. Demonstrate different types of phrasing.

2. Demonstrate three-quarter time by tapping a pencil.

3. Transpose this piece from the key of C to the key of G.

4. Play this piece of music.

94

VALUES LEVEL

1. Write your own music and play it.

2. Interpret someone else's music by playing it in your own way.

3. Play your instrument to suit a mood or to accomplish some goal (rather than simply to practice).

4. Consider and discuss these values questions:

• Did you choose the instrument you now play? Did you have a reason for choosing it?

• What do you like most about practicing? What do you like least?

• When do you practice? When do you play for fun? Do you ever play just to let off steam?

• Do you prefer to play an instrument by yourself or with others in an orchestra or small ensemble?

• If you were an accomplished musician, what kind of music would you be playing?

• Do you like to perform for others? How does performing make you feel?

Music Appreciation

FACTS LEVEL

1. Who composed *Madame Butterfly?*

2. Name three jazz musicians and the instruments they play.

3. Name the members of the woodwind family.

4. What is the difference between a sonata and a sonatina?

5. Here are some pieces of music we've studied. What is the name of each piece? Who composed each piece? When was each piece composed?

CONCEPTS LEVEL

1. By listening, tell whether each piece (or parts of the whole work) is written in a major or minor key.

2. Listen to this piece of music and tell what instruments are playing.

3. Compare and contrast the rock opera *Tommy* with *Madame Butterfly*. How does the music express the lyrics in each?

4. What are the differences between early American folk songs and old English folk songs? What do the

96

differences represent?

5. Think of a piece that contains syncopated rhythm.

6. Here are some musical compositions similar to others we have heard. See if you can identify the composer and the period.

VALUES LEVEL

1. What does this piece of music say to you? How does it make you feel? (What do the words mean to you?)

2. Rank the following five pieces of music in order of most liked to least liked. Can you identify what it is about each selection that accounts for your ranking?

3. Do you listen to records? If so, what does listening to records do for you? What meaning has it for your life?

4. Have you ever wanted to play a musical instrument? If so, which one? Would you consider taking lessons? What musical accomplishment of yours are you proud of?

5. If you were going to a rock concert, name the three friends you would like to go with you. Do you see these people often? Would you go to a concert alone? What are your reasons?

6. Does music affect your moods? Do your moods

affect the music you play? Play a record and move freely to the music. What feelings did your movements reflect?

7. Describe the atmosphere you prefer for the following types of music: jazz, rock, folk, classical.

8. What part does music play in your life? Would you like it to play a greater part in your life? If so, try to make a plan to accomplish this. Let us know if it works out.

9. Can you think of a song whose lyrics you especially like? Do these lyrics have any meaning for your life? Discuss.

10. Can you think of three pieces of the same style of music which you really like? Will you bring one of these in to play for the class and explain why you like it?

Other areas where music can be considered on the values level are: the social implications of rock and folk music; an appreciation of ethnic heritages; religion and music; marching songs and peace songs; etc. Music teachers may get other ideas by looking at the preceding section on Art.

RELIGION

St. Francis of Assisi

FACTS LEVEL

1. What was St. Francis's real name? Where and when was he born?

2. What events led to the rejection by St. Francis of his old life style? What were his father's reactions?

3. What kind of clothes did St. Francis wear? What did his clothes represent?

4. Why is St. Francis almost always pictured with birds nearby?

5. How did St. Francis die?

CONCEPTS LEVEL

1. In the early thirteenth century, when St. Francis lived, he claimed that he was married to "Lady Poverty." Why was this such an unorthodox statement for a man of God to make at that time? What else was unorthodox about St. Francis?

2. Pope Innocent III was faced with a dilemma when dealing with St. Francis. What were some of the issues surrounding the pope's problem with St. Francis?

3. How do you explain the rapid increase in the number of friars?

4. St. Francis literally worked himself to death, and even upon dying, he thanked God. Can you explain that?

5. What contribution did St. Francis make to the church, and why does he earn a place in its history?

VALUES LEVEL

1. How near do poor families live to you? How much concern should you have about poverty? Have you ever done anything about poverty? Can anything be done? By whom?

2. Do you know your own father well enough to predict his reaction if you were to live as St. Francis did? Explain.

3. Have you ever worn clothes that your group considered daring? If so, what happened to you? What did your friends and family say? If you haven't, how would you feel if you found yourself in a situation where your clothes were different from everyone else's? What do clothes mean to you?

4. St. Francis and Pope Innocent were able to understand and appreciate one another. If you were able to talk with the current pope, what would you discuss

with him? What direction would you urge him to take in his capacity as an important religious leader? Will you consider writing a letter to him?

5. Have you ever tried to communicate with an authority, for example, your teacher or your principal? What happened? How did you feel? What would you have done differently? If you were able to communicate with your principal, what direction would you urge him to take in administering your school?

6. Today many men also work themselves to death. Others may have ulcers or smoke or drink too much because of their work. What does that say to you about your own life?

Almost any topic in religion can be taught on all three levels.

BOOKKEEPING

FACTS LEVEL

1. What is a debit?

2. Name the steps necessary to make a payroll.

3. What is the correct bank balance for this set of information?

CONCEPTS LEVEL

1. What is the difference between a balance sheet and a profit and loss statement?

2. What is the purpose of an audit?

3. What methods are there for keeping track of inventories? What would be some consequences of a firm having no method?

4. Compare double-entry and single-entry bookkeeping, noting the advantages and disadvantages of each.

VALUES LEVEL

1. What aspects of bookkeeping give you the most pleasure? The least pleasure?

2. How much effort do you exert to keep account of

your possessions? Is there a simple way to keep better accounts? Will you try it?

3. Can you envision any circumstances in which you would steal from a company? Would you ever embezzle funds?

4. Keep records of your income and expenditures for a period of time. Discuss the expenditures that gave you real pleasure and those that were not pleasurable. Are there any reasons why this was so? Did any expenditure prove disappointing? If so, can you learn something from that? How much was spent on yourself? On others? Would you like to change this proportion? How much of your income was earned? Unearned? How important is it that you work for your money?

5. Would you like to work as a bookkeeper? Doing what kind of work? How important is advancement to you? Would you prefer a challenge or certainty of success? Do you prefer working alone or with others? Would you work for a firm that was engaged in work which you disapproved of?

TYPING AND SHORTHAND

Material for typing or dictation might include selections containing provocative ideas, unusual values, or perplexing choices people sometimes face. Then, after the typing or shorthand exercise, students could discuss briefly the content in small or large groups. Or they could type or write in shorthand and post their ideas for others to read. Almost any values-clarification strategies that require writing are adaptable to typing and shorthand classes. They can be found in the books *Values and Teaching* (30) and *Values-Clarification: A Handbook of Practical Strategies* (37) as well as in other sections of this chapter.

The typing and shorthand teacher might also raise the following discussion questions and activities for consideration by the class.

1. What goal do you have that skills such as typing and shorthand can help you attain?

2. What responsibilities would you most prefer to have at a job?

3. What office practices would you set up if you headed a secretarial pool? Share your reasons.

4. Using the correct format, type a letter to the editor of your town or school newspaper expressing your views on a current issue. Would you consider sending the letter?

5. Rank these jobs in terms of desirability and explain your ranking.

    a. private secretary
    b. member of a secretarial pool
    c. combination secretary and receptionist
    d. clerk-typist
    e. administrative assistant

6. Discuss the use of office supplies for personal use. Discuss the use of office time for personal phone calls or letter writing.

7. Consider the purpose of the business you would work for. Would you work for a firm that did anything? Where would you draw the line?

8. What would be the best employer-employee relationship for you? How personal? How permanent? Would you prefer to be unionized?

9. How would you like your boss to evaluate your work? How point out mistakes? (Students might role-play this question.)

Beyond
The Third Level

WHAT IS WORTH TEACHING?

A fifth-grade teacher has read *Clarifying Values through Subject Matter.* Now he or she is inspired. He comes into class the next day and says, "Boys and girls, I have an exciting lesson planned for today. Yesterday, you recall, we learned about the seven major products of Argentina. Well, today, we are going to think about how this subject area relates to *our own values.* I have a few questions for you:

1. How do you feel about the seven major products of Argentina?
2. Rank the seven products in order of your preferences.
3. Would you be willing to write a letter to the editor with your views on the seven major products of Argentina?"

What is worth teaching?

Much of what is taught in schools is so remote from students' lives that it would be a travesty to try to teach that material on the values level. Sugar-coating an irrelevant curriculum with values questions is not the way to clarify and develop values. It will fool no one for very long.

Therefore, before teachers begin to find ways to

teach their subject area on the values level, they must ask themselves some serious questions:
- Why am I teaching this subject area?
- Do I really believe my students need to have this knowledge or these skills?
- If I had no restraints or mandates imposed on me, what would I freely choose to teach?
- How does each area I am considering teaching relate to my students' lives?
- What are the real values dilemmas present in the subjects and themes I teach?

There is no foolproof way of determining what to include in a curriculum or what to eliminate from it. Each teacher must reach this decision on his own, and very likely, this will be an ongoing decision.

Many teachers will continue to teach subject matter which they regard as valuable, even if it has no apparent relation to how students live their lives. To teach with a focus on values does not mean to eliminate these areas from the curriculum. It is a question of balance. Each teacher must decide which areas of his subject he will teach in order to focus on values and which areas of his subject he will teach for other purposes.

It is the responsibility of teachers, administrators, and schools to make these decisions. As educators, we believe schools have neglected teaching with a focus on values. Hopefully, as more teachers feel the urgency for values-clarification, they will create a balance in their own teaching of facts, concepts, and values. As this happens, we will undoubtedly see major changes in curricula as well.

If the three-level concept helps to make standard subject matter more interesting and more relevant, fine. But, ideally, teachers will refuse to settle for "standard subject matter." Hopefully, they will build more of their curricula around skills and subjects which play an integral part in their students' lives.

Values Units

When teachers do begin to ask themselves the question "What is worth teaching?" their answer is frequently "values units."

A values unit is one which focuses on values, and the subject matter and skills to be taught are selected specifically to contribute to values deliberations.

Here is an example of a values unit used with a high school English class by one of the authors.

Based on the author's own values and his past experience with students, he felt that an important values issue for teenagers was the question of man and God, through the themes of: the meaning of life; life and death; and religion.

Before he began to choose the subject matter, he had a values goal in mind. The author wanted his students to become aware of what they prized and cherished, to examine and weigh the pros and cons of alternative ideas, to choose their own beliefs and behaviors, and to bring their actions into harmony with their beliefs.

The teacher selected the subject matter with a

view toward facilitating the major goal of applying the valuing process to the subject of man and God. He chose five literary works, each with a different perspective on the theme of man and God. Thus, students were given alternative viewpoints to examine. The selected literature was *Oedipus Rex* by Sophocles, the *Book of Job* from the Bible, *The Rubaiyat of Omar Khayyam*, *Crime and Punishment* by Fyodor Dostoyevsky, and *The Plague* by Albert Camus.

After the main purpose of the values unit was explained, the students read and discussed all five pieces of literature until they understood it on the facts and concepts levels. Then the students began to examine the values questions, probing the literature as it pertained to their own lives, exploring in depth what they believed or didn't believe, defending their beliefs in class, and making their own choices about the part God and religion would or wouldn't play in their lives.

Almost every segment of the values unit was taught on all three levels.

Literary analysis and writing skills were developed, but the focus of the analysis and writing was always on values also. For example, in the unit, the following concept questions were asked:

• If Omar Khayyam were living today, which would he most likely be?
>   a. a university philosophy professor
>   b. a hard-working business executive
>   c. a hippie

• Where was Job on the following continuum at the

109

beginning of the book? Where was he at the end of the book?

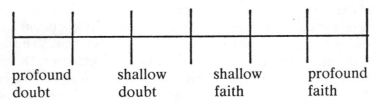

profound   shallow   shallow   profound
doubt   doubt   faith   faith

While literary analysis took place on the concepts level, students needed to return to the facts level to support their opinions. From that point the shift to the values level was relatively simple:

• Which of these persons are you most like now? Which might you be most like ten years from now?

• At what point on the continuum are you now? Where were you three years ago? Where do you think you'll be three years from now?

Whereas third-level teaching starts with a given subject that is taken to the values level, the values unit begins on the values level, and the subject matter is selected to help develop the goals of values-clarification.

Values units can be created in almost any subject area. In a chemistry class, ecology may be the values issue that is the focus of the unit. The unit may involve hearing and weighing arguments about phosphate pollution and may result in a campaign to clean up a local river. But uninformed action is not good citizenship,

110

nor would it be good science teaching. In order for students to act responsibly, they would have to know chemistry—perhaps the periodic table, how to analyze solutions, how compounds are formed, or the chemistry of photosynthesis. Thus the facts and concepts are learned after all, but not because they are part of the curriculum and have to be "covered." Rather, facts and concepts are learned because they are necessary to enable students to clarify and act on their values.

At present, the creation of values units in the various subject areas is a major thrust of the new work being done in values-clarification. Most such units begin with the challenge of a real values problem.

Values Strategies

As part of the values-clarification approach, over a hundred methods, activities, or "strategies" have been developed to help students build the processes of prizing, choosing, and acting into their lives. These strategies—like Values Voting, Rank Ordering, and the Values Continuum—are described in *Values and Teaching* (30) and *Values Clarification: A Handbook of Practical Strategies* (37). Values strategies usually do not require a change in a teacher's approach to subject matter. Rather, they can be used briefly, to enliven a class, change the pace, or fill free time, while still contributing importantly to student value-growth.

At some point in a student's education, however, the subject should be the student himself and his developing values, questions, and concerns. Whether

111

this is achieved in separate courses (as more and more schools are doing) or in separate parts of a course or day, the teacher should not have to search for ways to lift traditional subject matter to the values level. At this point, the values level should be the only level and the values strategies an integral part of the course.

Values strategies can also be used in connection with traditional subject matter. There are several examples of values strategies pertaining to traditional subjects throughout this book. Teachers who are familiar with many of the strategies will find numerous applications of the strategies to their subjects.

One of the strategies is the Public Interview, in which the teacher asks one student a series of questions about his beliefs, opinions, and activities. After a teacher has conducted several interviews on general values issues, he can then use the public interview with the subject matter. A history teacher might ask a student to be interviewed as Abraham Lincoln. The student would answer questions about slavery, marriage, politics, or city versus country living just as he thinks Lincoln would have answered. Then, on the values level, he would give his own opinions on the same values questions. A science teacher might have a student portray a famous scientist being interviewed about his life's work; for example, Mendel on genetics or Madame Curie on the discovery of radiation.

Almost all of the values-clarification strategies can similarly be used to help teach the subject matter on all three levels. The following chapter provides numerous examples of this approach.

Self-Directed Learning

Throughout this book, it has been assumed that the teacher makes the decisions about what subject areas will be taught and how they will be taught. This assumption was made because, in many of our schools, the teacher is still making most of the decisions and probably will be making them for some time to come. But much of the exciting work being done in education today allows *students* to make decisions and choices about their education.

Student choice has appeared in a variety of major ways. Among these are:

The open classroom. In this situation, the classroom is an environment rich in learning resources. The individual students, operating within certain structures and guidelines, choose how they will spend their time. The teacher serves as a "facilitator" of learning, working as helper, aide, and consultant to students, but not as the director of everyone's time and energy. The open classroom has been most frequently used on the primary and elementary levels, but it is spreading to other levels as well.

Group planning. Here, the class as a whole sets curricular goals for itself and works toward those goals. Or a class divides into subgroups and each subgroup selects its own goal. The teacher often helps as a group-process consultant (32) and as a teacher of

113

discussion and research skills. Teachers who use the "core curriculum" often teach in this style.

Choice of subjects. With this approach, within the limitations of state requirements, students make significant choices as to the classes they will take. Required subjects are kept at a minimum, and students decide which subjects will best enhance their growth and help them achieve their goals. To use the approach productively, a good advising system is important. This approach is an extention of the open classroom idea, but the entire school is the environment rich in resources.

Student control. Sometimes students will sit on policy-making boards, and in varying degrees, influence important school-wide decisions such as the selection of subjects to be offered. This is an alternative to teacher-controlled subject matter.

All of the educational alternatives described have profound implications for the way students learn. They are consistent with the valuing process, for they allow students to examine alternatives and weigh consequences—to make their own choices. Therefore, student-directed learning is another viable way, beyond values-level teaching, to focus on values. Carl Rogers' *Freedom to Learn* (31) is an important resource in the area of student-centered learning.

Humanistic Education

Teaching on the facts, concepts, and values levels is not the only way to bridge the gap between subject matter and students' lives. Within the movement known variously as humanistic, psychological, affective, or confluent education, there are several other approaches that have similar process goals (1, 2, 4, 5, 6, 9, 10, 27, 32, 39). In order not to change the focus of this discussion, these other approaches will not be examined here; but they are important to mention in the context of this chapter. The prospect of integrating these approaches with the work in values-clarification is an exciting one.

Using
The Values
Strategies
With Subject Matter

This chapter, written by Clifford E. Knapp,* provides fifteen values strategies that can be used to clarify values through subject matter. Knapp's subject is environmental education. However, these strategies can be adapted to almost every subject in the curriculum. They would be used in conjunction with facts- and concepts-level teaching. The following values strategies are used:

1. Value Sheets

2. Voting

3. Role Playing

4. Rank Ordering

*Clifford E. Knapp, Outdoor Education/Science Specialist, Ridgewood Public Schools, Ridgewood, New Jersey. These sections are reprinted from two articles (24, 25).

5. Contrived Incidents

6. Picture Without a Caption

7. Values Continuum

8. Coded Papers

9. Devil's Advocate

10. Autobiographical Questionnaire

11. Time Diary

12. Unfinished Sentences

13. Conflict Story

14. Sensitivity Modules

15. Value-Clarifying Discussions

Value Sheets

A Value Sheet consists of a thought-provoking statement or quotation followed by a series of value-eliciting questions for the students to respond to. Value sheets can also be composed of questions based on a film, play, or other experience that has been shared by the students. The following are two examples of a Value Sheet.

117

EXAMPLE:

"People like to make money. If more profit can be made by polluting the earth, people will pollute. If more profit can be made by replacing an old machine, it will be thrown away. Increased profit has been the main reason for our high standard of living in the United States. Everybody is for making the environment a better place until it costs them more money. If pollution control causes a person to lose his job or causes him any inconvenience, he is not for it."

To think and write on:

• Do you agree with the author's point of view about people and what they seem to value most?

• Can you think of five things you value even more than money? List them.

• What percentage of your allowance (income) would you be willing to give to improving the environment?

• If you had to give up five electrical appliances or machines in your house to cut down on pollution, which would be the five easiest to do without?

• How would you feel if a new law was passed requiring you and your family to reduce electricity usage by one-third? Would you do this without a law?

118

EXAMPLE:

*"Our society depends upon man's ability to change
the natural environment."*

To think and write on:

• How has man changed the natural environment in
your community? (For example, planted lawns, built
roads, cleared land for shopping centers.)

• Which changes in the environment do you think
were good and which were bad for your community?
Consider both short-term and long-term effects.

• If you could make a change in your community's
environment, what would you change? What would
the consequences be?

• Is this something you'd like to work on? What would
your first steps have to be?

Voting

The teacher asks questions which require the
students to take a stand on issues by raising their
hands. The purpose of voting is to direct the students'
attention to a problem that they may not have thought
much about. The teacher should vote too.

• How many use lead-free gas in your family car?

• How many have ever thrown a piece of paper on the
ground and left it?

119

- How many have passed litter without picking it up?

- How many have purchased nonreturnable bottles during the last week?

- How many have refused to buy something because it had excess packaging?

- How many have refused to have their purchases placed in a paper bag at the store in order to conserve paper?

Role Playing
Describe a situation which presents different viewpoints on an issue and have the students assume the roles of the individuals involved. Role Playing can point out a need for further study of an issue in order to better understand the facts.

EXAMPLE:
The following letter was written to a college newspaper in 1970:

To the Daily Egyptian:
When spring arrives this year, an indefensibly cruel scene will be reenacted on the coasts of the Northwest Atlantic and Gulf of St. Lawrence. Every spring and summer, thousands of baby seals are brutally slaughtered by Canadian and Norwegian hunters. The single

120

purpose of these mass killings is to collect seal pelts, which are made into fur clothing.

Whatever dubious justification exists for killing innocent creatures solely for their fur, there certainly can be no defensible excuse for the manner in which these seals are murdered. The hunters club and skin them, in many cases while they are still conscious. Last spring alone, 260,000 baby seals were killed this way. The United States government, on whose soil this barbarism is taking place, has failed to put an end to the manner in which these animals are being destroyed.

Sue Carruthers
Graduate student
Government

Have students play the roles of the letter writer, a seal hunter, a United States government official, and officials from Canada and Norway.

EXAMPLE:
At a city council meeting, an ordinance to ban the sale of nonreturnable beverage containers is to be voted upon. Before the vote is taken, the mayor reads letters received from three concerned citizens.

Dear Mayor:
As a consumer, I urge that the council defeat the proposed ordinance that would ban the sale of nonreturnable beverage containers in the city. Many of my favorite drinks are not available in anything but

throw-away bottles or cans. It would be an inconvenience for me to drive to the next town to buy them there. Besides, this is supposed to be a "free country." This law would take away my freedom to buy the beverages I like in my home town.

Signed,
Bert Crust

Dear Mayor:

Please tell the city council to vote for the ordinance to ban nonreturnable beverage containers. As you know, we have a litter problem in the city, and the ban would reduce it considerably. Besides, it costs less to buy drinks in returnable containers. Our city should be a leader in doing something about our nation's refuse problem.

Signed,
Betty Smith

Dear Mayor:

As a member of the Chamber of Commerce, I would like to voice my opposition to the proposed law to ban the sale of nonreturnable bottles and cans. Many people in our community will drive to neighboring towns to purchase nonreturnables. Our businesses will suffer from the ordinance and some people will lose their jobs and be inconvenienced. Please vote "no" on this issue.

Signed,
Philip Harding

122

Role-play the city council meeting having the students take the positions of the letter writers and other interested citizens.

Rank Ordering

Words or statements are placed on the blackboard and the students are asked to rank them in order of their preference. Rank Ordering can lead to discussions of why different students have varying preferences. Here are examples of Rank Ordering.

Given a small budget to spend on the litter problem in your community, how would you rank the following proposals to spend the money?
• Purchase litter containers.
• Place "No Littering" signs in strategic places.
• Hire someone to pick up litter.

If you had the money to purchase machinery to recycle only one type of material, how would you rank the following in importance in your community?
      a. paper
      b. glass
      c. aluminum

Your city owns a thousand acres on the edge of town. How would you rank the following land uses?
• Lease the land to a strip mining company with the understanding that the city would share in some of the profits and the company would reclaim the land.

123

- Sell the land to a large department store for development of a shopping center.
- Lease the land for grazing.

Contrived Incidents

The teacher can create situations which stimulate discussion of controversial environmental issues.

For example, the teacher can take the students on a short walk on the school grounds during which the teacher casually throws a piece of paper on the ground and walks away. The teacher could also break a limb from a tree or write on the school building with chalk. A guest speaker could be invited into the classroom to disagree with the teacher on an environmental issue. After the incidents, the students can discuss their thoughts and feelings.

Picture Without a Caption

Have the students write a caption to a picture depicting an environmental problem. The caption may reveal the students' values about particular environmental problems. Divide the students into small groups and provide an opportunity for them to share their captions. Ask them if they learned something about their environmental values and those of others in the classroom.

Values Continuum

The teacher can construct an environmental Value Continuum and place it on the chalkboard. Have the students go to the board in turn and place a mark on the line indicating their position. Have them indicate some of the reasons for selecting their position.

What is your position on these value lines?

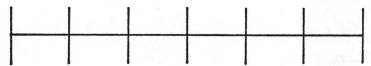

Returnable Ron	No-deposit Norris
He uses only returnable containers and will not eat or drink anything that comes in a throw-away container.	He uses only nonreturn-able containers because he thinks that return-ables are too much trouble to take back.

Bike-riding Betty	Motoring Mable
She doesn't use any vehicles that pollute the air and therefore rides her bike to work forty miles away each day.	She uses motor vehicles every chance she gets. She even retrieves the evening paper by taking the car down the drive-way of her home.

125

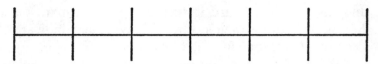

Pure-air Paul   Polluted Polly

He is so opposed to air   She is so uncaring about
pollution that he takes   air pollution that she
short breaths so he   burns cigarettes for in-
won't add as much car-   cense.
bon dioxide to the air.

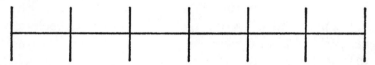

Let-live Larry   Pesticide Pete

He is so against any   He uses pesticides so
type of pesticide that   freely that he sprays his
he allows mosquitoes to   house and back yard
bite him rather than   daily to get rid of in-
spray them.   sects.

Coded Papers

The teacher or students can code papers with
pluses or minuses indicating what the writer is for
(plus) or against (minus). The papers can be written
by the students, and the teacher can do the coding
instead of assigning a letter grade. The students can
also code papers to indicate where they agree and

disagree with the author. This technique is also useful in analyzing environment articles which appear in newspapers and magazines. Students can more clearly determine the writer's values and understand why a certain position is taken on an issue.

EXAMPLE:
Place pluses next to words or phrases that you agree with and minuses next to words or phrases that you disagree with.

A Conservationist's Lament

The world is finite, resources are scarce,
Things are bad and will be worse.
Coal is burned and gas exploded,
Forests cut and soils eroded.
Wells are dry and air's polluted,
Dust is blowing, trees uprooted.
Oil is going, ores depleted,
Drains receive what is excreted.
Land is sinking, seas are rising,
Man is far too enterprising.
Fire will rage with Man to fan it,
Soon we'll have a plundered planet.
People breed like fertile rabbits,
People have disgusting habits.
Moral:
      The evolutionary plan
      Went astray by evolving Man.

The Technologist's Reply

Man's potential is quite terrific,
You can't go back to the Neolithic.
The cream is there for us to skim it,
Knowledge is power, and the sky's the limit.
Every mouth has hands to feed it,
Food is found when people need it.
All we need is found in granite
Once we have the men to plan it.
Yeast and algae give us meat,
Soil is almost obsolete.
Men can grow to pastures greener
Till all the earth is Pasadena.
Moral:

> Man's a nuisance, Man's a crackpot,
> But only Man can hit the jackpot.

Kenneth Boulding

Devil's Advocate

The teacher can develop plausible reasons defending various pollution practices and attempt to justify that position to the students.

EXAMPLE:

The teacher could state reasons why a chemical factory *should be allowed* to continue to dump waste into a river. Some plausible reasons could be:

• It keeps the cost of the chemical products low.

128

- The industry could not compete with other chemical industries if it had to build expensive waste treatment facilities.

- Rivers have been used to dispose of wastes for centuries.

- Most of the public doesn't really care if the dumping continues.

After the short talk justifying certain kinds of pollution, the teacher should encourage discussion of the topic.

Autobiographical Questionnaire
The teacher can construct questions which will examine the students' behavior in regard to environmental pollution.

Have you ever:

- thrown refuse on the ground or in the water?

- picked up litter from the ground?

- burned trash outside?

- reported a violation of a fish or game law?

- donated time or money to an environmental organization?

- fixed a leaking water fixture immediately?

• asked your mother to change her laundry detergent to a less harmful one?

• written a letter to the editor protesting a misuse of the environment?

• written a letter to a government official expressing your position on an environmental issue?

Students write, then talk about, any time(s) they have done these activities. In this way, students hear from their peers alternatives for environmental action which they might want to build into their own lives.

Time Diary
The student is asked to keep a record of how he spends his time for one week. A Time Diary is a chart listing what a person does every hour or half-hour during the week. It should be stressed that this is a private diary that the teacher will not read. After completion of the diary, the students are asked to respond to such questions as:

• What have you done this week, if anything, that might have contributed to pollution?

• What have you done this week, if anything, that might have made your environment a better place in which to live?

• How many hours did you spend which involved the use of electricity? If you wanted to, how could you reduce this amount of time next week? Do you want to?

• In general, are you proud of (do you feel good about) how you used your time this week?

Unfinished Sentences
An unfinished sentence is written on the chalkboard and the students are asked to respond in writing. Student responses may indicate some of the values which they believe to be important.

"If I had the power to correct one environmental problem, I would choose...."

"The best way to reduce noise in my community is to...."

"The school grounds could be made more beautiful by...."

"I would rather live with a little pollution than...."

"All of the attention paid to pollution in the newspapers and on television is...."

"The laws regulating pollution should be...."

Conflict Story (Sometimes called "Alligator River")
Read the following story and then list the names of the characters according to whom you liked the most and whom you liked least. Discuss the lists after completing them. Try to describe some of the values

you think each man may hold. Have the students discuss how the situation could be resolved.

The Ajax Paper Company was dumping poisonous chemicals into a stream, causing the fish to die and the water to become smelly and polluted. Mr. Pedigrew, president of the company, knew that the fishing, swimming, and tourist businesses were suffering, but pollution control would have cost the company a lot of money. The company employed about half of the town's residents and doing something about the problem would mean that most of them might have to be fired. Mr. Chambers, chairman of the town's chamber of commerce and long-time friend of Mr. Pedigrew, wanted to bring more tourists to the area, but didn't want to report the pollution because of the already high unemployment in the area. Mr. Chambers wanted instead to develop another amusement park to attract more tourists as well as to provide more jobs. Mr. Barnum, owner of the only amusement park in the area, feared the competition of another amusement attraction and reported the polluting paper company to state environmental control officials. The company was closed down and the employees were put out of work. Mr. Townsend, mayor of the town, sympathized with the families of the unemployed workers and wrote a letter to the state to try to reopen the paper company even though it would still pollute the stream. Mr. Moneybags, owner of a large summer resort, became so angry with the mayor's attempt to reopen the paper company that he withdrew his support for a community

132

park that the mayor was promoting, making it impossible to complete the project.

Sensitivity Modules
• Make a survey of how foods are packaged for sale. Bring in samples of packaging which seem to be excessive and wasteful. Why do manufacturers sometimes use packaging which appears to waste materials? How much refuse could be eliminated if products were packaged differently? Display your findings on posters. What would happen if people didn't buy products that had excess packaging?

• Have the students design a vehicle for a family to use in the city. They should consider such factors as air pollution, size of vehicle, how to park it, and where it should travel (above or below ground) in the city. How does each design reflect the student's values?

Value-Clarifying Discussions
• Conduct a panel discussion or debate concerning the question of whether drilling for oil under water should be continued in certain areas. Also discuss placing oil pipes above ground as some oil companies propose in Alaska. Consider the viewpoints of the oil companies, ecologists, local citizens, and government officials.

• Conduct a classroom discussion about the pros and cons of completely eradicating a particular pest. If students assume opposing viewpoints, the discussion

133

will serve to help clarify their values about the environment. Examine specific animals such as the mosquito, Japanese beetle, elm bark beetle, bag worm, tick, flea, chigger, aphid, blister beetle, and boll weevil. Examine plants such as poison ivy, ragweed, and poison sumac. Which ones will affect the ecology of an area least if they are completely eradicated? Does the whole class agree that a particular plant or animal is a pest?

• Discuss Ogden Nash's poem:

Song of the Open Road

I think that I shall never see
A billboard as lovely as a tree
Indeed, unless the billboards fall,
I'll never see a tree at all.

Did the poet really mean that he'd never see a tree as long as billboards are there? If he were a businessman who depended upon the tourists who saw the sign, would he feel the same way? Write a poem about billboards from a businessman's point of view. Write a poem of your own about the environment.

These, then, are some ways of using values-clarification strategies to elevate the teaching of subject matter to the values level.

A Three-Level Review for You

We could, of course, ask you some **facts-level** questions about the book:

• Name and define the three levels.

• Give three examples the book used to illustrate subject matter on the *values* level.

• True or False: The position this book takes is that there is no room in schools for facts-level teaching.

• Spell the authors' names correctly.

Alternately, we could pose some **concepts-level** questions to assess your understanding of the ideas presented in the book and to see how they relate to other ideas you are familiar with.

• Give the thesis of the book in less than one page.

• Develop some facts, concepts, and values-level questions or strategies which you might use in a unit on the war in Vietnam. Now develop the same types of questions or strategies for use with the digestive system.

• Consider the impacts three different teachers would probably have on students if the teachers were distinguished by the level of subject matter each concentrated on: Mr. Facts, Mr. Concepts, and Mr. Values. What might be the reactions of principals to these three teachers? Of parents? Of students when, as adults, they look back on their schooling?

• What are some alternative methods of analyzing subject matter (or alternative approaches to "humanize" education)? How are they related to the three-level concept of teaching?

As you might expect, we hope that readers will also review the book in light of **values-level** questions:

• What did you like best about this book?

• What did you find was its biggest shortcoming?

• Consider a subject area (or unit) you now teach or are preparing to teach. Develop facts-, concepts-, and values-level questions or activities which could be used in teaching this subject area. Which of these questions or activities are you likely to use?

• Take any two of the values strategies used in the chapter on environmental education and adapt them to fit a subject or unit you now teach or will teach. Would you like to try these out with your students?

• What percentage of time do you wish your teachers in elementary school had devoted to each of the three levels? Would you have wished for the same percentages in high school? In college?

• Has this book changed the way you look at subject matter? If so, how? Can you tell if any change will be lasting? How do you know?

• What, if anything, do you predict you will do differently about teaching now that you have been introduced to the three-level scheme? How do you feel about those predicted actions (or inactions)?

Bibliography

1. Alschuler, Alfred, ed. *Psychological Humanistic Education.* A special issue of *Educational Opportunity Forum.* Albany, New York: State Department of Education, Fall, 1969.

2. Alschuler, Alfred; Tabor, Diane; and McIntyre, James. *Teaching Achievement Motivation.* Middletown, Connecticut: Education Ventures, Inc., 1970.

3. Bloom, Benjamin S., ed. *Taxonomy of Educational Objectives, Handbook I: Cognitive Domain.* New York: David McKay Co., 1965.

4. Borton, Terry. *Reach, Touch and Teach.* New York: McGraw-Hill, 1970.

5. Borton, Terry, and Newberg, Norman. *Education for Student Concerns.* New York: McGraw-Hill, in press.

6. Brown, George I. *Human Teaching for Human Learning.* New York: Viking Press, 1971.

7. Bruner, Jerome S. *The Process of Education.* Cambridge, Massachusetts: Harvard University Press, 1960.

8. Dewey, John. *Experience and Education.* New York: The Macmillan Co., 1963.

9. Glasser, William. *Schools Without Failure.* New York: Harper and Row, 1969.

10. Gordon, Thomas. *Parent Effectiveness Training: The No-Lose Program for Raising Responsible Children.* New York: Peter H. Wyden, Inc., 1970.

11. Harmin, Merrill, and Simon, Sidney B. "The Subject Matter Controversy Revisited." *Peabody Journal of Education,* vol. 42, no. 4, January, 1965.

12. Harmin, Merrill, and Simon, Sidney B. "Subject Matter with a Focus on Values." *Educational Leadership,* vol. 26, no. 1, October, 1968.

13. Harmin, Merrill; Kirschenbaum, Howard; and Simon, Sidney B. "Teaching History with a Focus on Values." *Social Education,* vol. 33, no. 5, May, 1969.

14. Harmin, Merrill; Kirschenbaum, Howard; and Simon, Sidney B. "Teaching Science with a Focus on Values." *The Science Teacher,* vol. 37, no. 1, January, 1970.

15. Harmin, Merrill, and Simon, Sidney B. "Values." In *Teacher's Handbook,* edited by Dwight W. Allen and Eli Seifman. Glenview, Illinois: Scott, Foresman & Co., 1971.

16. Harmin, Merrill; Kirschenbaum, Howard; and Simon, Sidney B. "The Search for Values with a Focus on Math."

In *Teaching Mathematics in the Elementary School—What's Needed? What's Happening?* Washington, D.C.: National Association of Elementary School Principals and National Council of Teachers of Mathematics, 1970.

17. Kirschenbaum, Howard. "Teaching the Black Experience." *Educator's Guide to Media and Methods,* vol. 5, October, 1968.

18. Kirschenbaum, Howard. "The Free Choice English Curriculum." Upper Jay, New York: Adirondack Mt. Humanistic Education Center, 1969.

19. Kirschenbaum, Howard. "Sensitivity Modules." *Media and Methods,* vol. 6, February, 1970.

20. Kirschenbaum, Howard. "Teaching Home Economics with a Focus on Values." Upper Jay, New York: Adirondack Mt. Humanistic Education Center, 1971.

21. Kirschenbaum, Howard, and Simon, Sidney B. "Teaching English with a Focus on Values." *English Journal,* vol. 58, October, 1969.

22. Kirschenbaum, Howard; Napier, Rodney W.; and Simon, Sidney B. *WAD-JA-GET? The Grading Game in American Education.* New York: Hart Publishing Co., 1971.

23. Kohl, Herbert. *36 Children.* New York: New American Library, 1968.

24. Knapp, Clifford E. "Children Explore Their Values." *Instructor,* March, 1972.

25. Knapp, Clifford E. "Teaching Environmental Education with a Focus on Values." Upper Jay, New York: Adirondack Mt. Humanistic Education Center, 1972.

26. Krathwohl, David; Bloom, Benjamin; and Masia, Bertram. *Taxonomy of Educational Objectives, Handbook II: Affective Domain.* New York: David McKay Co., 1964.

27. Lyon, Harold C., Jr. *Learning to Feel—Feeling to Learn, Humanistic Education for the Whole Man.* Columbus, Ohio: Charles E. Merrill, 1971.

28. Neill, A.S. *Summerhill: A Radical Approach to Child Rearing.* New York: Hart Publishing Co., 1960.

29. Postman, Neil, and Weingartner, Charles. *Teaching as a Subversive Activity.* New York: Delacorte Press, 1969.

30. Raths, Louis E.; Harmin, Merrill; and Simon, Sidney B. *Values and Teaching: Working with Values in the Classroom.* Columbus, Ohio: Charles E. Merrill, 1966.

31. Rogers, Carl R. *Freedom to Learn: A View of What Education Might Become.* Columbus, Ohio: Charles E. Merrill, 1969.

32. Schumuck, Richard, and Schumuck, Patricia. *Group Processes in the Classroom.* Dubuque, Iowa: William C. Brown, 1970.

33. Simon, Sidney B. "Three Ways to Teach Church School." *Colloquy,* January, 1970.

34. Simon, Sidney B. "Your Values Are Showing." *Colloquy,* January, 1970.

35. Simon, Sidney B. "Sensitizing Modules: A Cure for Senioritis." *Scholastic Teacher,* 21 September 1970.

36. Simon, Sidney B., and Carnes, Alice. "Teaching Afro-American History with a Focus on Values." *Educational Leadership,* vol. 27, December, 1969.

37. Simon, Sidney B.; Howe, Leland W.; and Kirschenbaum, Howard. *Values Clarification: A Handbook of Practical Strategies for Teachers and Students.* New York: Hart Publishing Co., 1972.

38. Warner, Sylvia Ashton. *Teacher.* New York: Simon and Schuster, 1963.

39. Weinstein, Gerald, and Fantini, Mario. *Toward Humanistic Education: A Curriculum of Affect.* New York: Praeger, 1970.

Workshops on the values-clarification approach are held nationwide throughout the year.
To receive a brochure
describing the workshops and a list
of materials available on the values-clarification approach, write to:

VALUES ASSOCIATES
Box 43
Amherst, Massachusetts 01002